# Stay on
# POINT

**Jack McBain**

## 2

DARAKWON

# Stay on
# POINT ②

---

**Author** Jack McBain
**Publisher** Chung Kyudo
**Editors** Kwak Bitna, Cho Sangik
**Designers** Park Bohee, Lee Seunghyun

First Published December 2018
By Darakwon Inc.
Darakwon Bldg., 211, Munbal-ro, Paju-si, Gyeonggi-do 10881
Republic of Korea

Tel. 82-2-736-2031 (Ext. 553)

Price ₩13,000
ISBN 978-89-277-0963-3  14740
     978-89-277-0961-9  14740 (set)
http://www.darakwon.co.kr

Main Book / Free MP3 Available Online
7 6 5 4 3 2 1        18 19 20 21 22

# Introduction

*Stay on Point 2* is the second book in a two-level series for English language learners interested in learning techniques of oral presentations. Not only is this book appropriate for intermediate-level students familiar with these concepts, but it also serves as a helpful guide for more advanced students interested in reviewing speechwriting basics. The information in this book is essential for any high school student, university student, or professional person who might at some point need to prepare and deliver a speech in English. The information found in this series will not only prove helpful to English language learners hoping to improve their oral presentation skills but will also offer a glimpse into Western culture and the norms and traditions associated with public speaking in the West.

*Stay on Point 2* contains twelve units, which cover a variety of topics. Each unit consists of language-building exercises, a new presentation skill, and an outline for students to follow as they craft oral presentations of their own. Students will learn how to speak to inform as well as how to speak to persuade. Students will encounter topics such as *Childhood Memories*, *Locations around the World*, and *Advertising*. By including topics in the book which are interesting and relevant to a student's life, we believe we can make the speechwriting process easier and more enjoyable.

*Stay on Point 2* is a speech-preparation textbook which includes the steps necessary to write and deliver a speech from a Western academic perspective. The step-by-step approach in this book allows students to craft and deliver high-quality academic speeches on a wide variety of topics. Each unit introduces readers to a new aspect of the speech-preparation process. As students come to the end of a unit, they will find that they have added another tool to their speechwriting toolkit. Each unit in the book gradually becomes more challenging as students are asked to apply knowledge they learned in the previous units to the current one. The vocabulary, language-learning, pronunciation, and reading sections give students a chance to improve their overall linguistic skills. Communicative tasks, such as pair work and class activities, provide students with opportunities to apply what they have learned in the language-building sections to authentic speaking situations. Each unit aims to help students build confidence and gain competence as they develop their oral presentation skills.

## Author's Acknowledgments

The author would like to express his most sincere gratitude to the editor Bitna Kwak. Without her tireless work and guidance, this project would not have been possible. He would also like to acknowledge the contributions of Mr. Michael Putlack and the entire Darakwon management and staff. Finally, he would like to extend a heartfelt thanks to his family, who has been incredibly patient during the writing process of this book.

# Scope and Sequence

| Unit | Learning Outcomes | Vocabulary |
|---|---|---|
| **Unit 1**<br>**Childhood Memories** p.8-15<br><br>Childhood Memories<br>The Beginning, Middle, and Ending<br>Details in the Story | Students can . . .<br>talk about childhood memories<br>describe feelings associated with childhood memories<br>use sequence words to tell a story<br>conduct a brainstorming session<br>prepare a narrative speech about a childhood memory | Descriptive adjectives<br>Sequence words |
| **Unit 2**<br>**Success** p.16-23<br><br>Words Related to Success<br>Defining Terms in a Speech<br>Subtopics Related to Success | Students can . . .<br>talk about a specific person victory<br>define terms in a speech<br>discuss success as it relates to different areas of their lives<br>use transitions in a speech<br>prepare a definitional speech about success | Words related to success<br>Definitional words<br>Different areas of a person's life |
| **Unit 3**<br>**How to Do Something** p.24-31<br><br>Using Nuanced Language<br>The Sequence of Events<br>The Steps in a Process | Students can . . .<br>describe or explain a process to an audience<br>use nuanced language to describe the benefits of a process<br>use sequence words while describing a process<br>use attention-getting openers in speeches | Words associated with doing activities such as changing a tire, putting out a fire, and buying a used car<br>Sequence words |
| **Unit 4**<br>**Locations around the World** p.32-39<br><br>Perceptions<br>Differences<br>Different Locations | Students can . . .<br>talk about how various topics are discussed in different parts of the world<br>provide a contrast between different locations<br>write a preview and summary of the main points in a speech<br>paraphrase sentences | Different parts of the world<br>Opposing views |
| **Unit 5**<br>**Past, Present, and Future** p.40-47<br><br>In the Past, Now, and in the Future<br>Compare and Contrast the Past, Present, and Future<br>Interesting Details about the Past and Present | Students can . . .<br>talk about how objects were in the past, how they are now, and how they might be in the future<br>discuss how objects have changed or not changed<br>write strong concluding remarks in a speech | Words related to time and time periods |
| **Unit 6**<br>**Problems and Solutions** p.48-55<br><br>Identifying Problems<br>Definitions<br>Solutions as Main Points | Students can . . .<br>identify societal problems and discuss them<br>operationally define the terms in a speech<br>create and use PowerPoint slides responsibly | Common societal problems |

| Grammar | Language Patterns | Pronunciation | Reading | Learning How | Do It Yourself |
|---|---|---|---|---|---|
| Regular and irregular past tense verbs | Sequence words to tell the beginning, middle, and ending of a story | Common reductions of *had to* and *have to* | Details in a story | Brainstorming with mind mapping, jotting down notes, and freewriting | Give a speech about a childhood memory |
| Gerunds and infinitives | Defining terms | Common reductions of *of a* and *of an* | Subtopics related to success | Transitions | Give a speech about your definition of success |
| Modal auxiliary verbs | Sequence words | /z/ and /dʒ/ sounds | How to perform the steps in a process | Attention-getting opener strategies | Give a speech about how to do something |
| Prepositions of place | Stating opposite ideas | Ending sound /d/ + beginning sound /j/ = /dʒ/ sound | Various topics as they relate to different locations | Preview of the main points and summary of the main points | Give a speech about how different countries or cultures view a specific topic |
| Future tense *will* and *be going to* | Compare and contrast the past and the present | Ending sound /t/ + beginning sound /j/ = /tʃ/ sound | How baseball has changed over the years | Concluding remarks | Give a speech on any topic by using a past, present, and future organizational pattern |
| Relative pronouns *who*, *which*, *where*, and *that* | Expressions for defining terms | /v/ and /w/ sounds | Poverty and possible solutions | Using PowerPoint slides responsibly | Give a speech in which you identify a problem and offer solutions |

| Unit | Learning Outcomes | Vocabulary |
|---|---|---|
| **Unit 7**<br>**Cause and Effect I**    p.56-63<br>Emotions<br>A Cause and Its Effects<br>The Benefits | Students can . . .<br>describe emotions linked to specific causes<br>describe a cause and its effects<br>provide good supporting details in a speech<br>use charts and graphs effectively | Words related to emotions |
| **Unit 8**<br>**Cause and Effect II**    p.64-71<br>Common Issues and Social Problems<br>An Effect and Its Causes<br>Main Causes | Students can . . .<br>identify common issues and social problems that affect their lives<br>link a number of causes to a specific effect<br>provide causes as main points in the body in a speech<br>use additional types of charts and graphs | Effects of common issues and social problems |
| **Unit 9**<br>**Group Presentations**    p.72-79<br>Vocabulary for Meetings<br>Debating within a Group<br>Rules for Successful Group Presentations | Students can . . .<br>use common terms related to meetings<br>learn to make compromises<br>learn language for having healthy discussions and debates in a group<br>follow a helpful set of rules when choosing a presentation group<br>choose roles in a group | Meetings |
| **Unit 10**<br>**Challenging a Historical Belief**<br>   p.80-87<br>Little-Known Historical Facts<br>Expressing Opposition to a Viewpoint<br>Challenging a Common Belief | Students can . . .<br>state facts that support a claim challenging a historical belief<br>express opposition to another person's viewpoint<br>provide evidence that supports their claim<br>cite sources in a speech | Words related to history |
| **Unit 11**<br>**Advertising**    p.88-95<br>Describing a Product<br>Visualizing the Future<br>Putting It All Together | Students can . . .<br>use good descriptive language when telling an audience about a product<br>help an audience visualize a future where they have purchased a product<br>give reasons to support their claim that the audience members' lives would be better with a specific product<br>use Monroe's Motivated Sequence | Words related to advertising products |
| **Unit 12**<br>**Making a Change**    p.96-103<br>Then and Now<br>Start Now or Stop Now<br>Follow Your Bliss | Students can . . .<br>talk about how they have changed certain behaviors in their lives<br>use good motivational language to affect change in the audience members' lives<br>give inspirational examples of people from their own lives who have made positive changes<br>write good concluding remarks in a persuasive speech | Words related to behaviors |

| Grammar | Language Patterns | Pronunciation | Reading | Learning How | Do It Yourself |
|---|---|---|---|---|---|
| The suffixes *-ment*, *-ion*, and *-ance* | Describing a cause and its effects | Diphthongs | The benefits of exercise | Using charts and graphs | Give a speech in which you describe a cause and its effects |
| *Too much / too many* | Connecting causes to a specific effect | /s/ and /ʃ/ sounds | The main causes for divorce | Using charts and graphs (continued) | Give a speech in which you describe an effect and its causes |
| The first conditional | Group debate and discussion | Question types and the correct intonations | Four simple rules for successful group presentations | Choosing roles in a group | Give a group presentation on a topic of your group's choice |
| Apostrophes to show possession | Expressing opposition to a viewpoint | /ɪ/ and /i/ sounds | Challenging common beliefs about Christopher Columbus | Citing sources in a speech | Give a speech in which you challenge an incorrect historical belief |
| The first conditional with various modal auxiliary verbs | Visualizing the future | Common reductions of *It'll* and *What'll* | Why you should buy an ergonomic chair | Using Monroe's Motivated Sequence | Give a speech in which you try to persuade the audience to buy a specific product |
| *Used to* | Language for motivating people to change | Common reductions of *but I...*, *and I...*, and *or I...* | An argument for following your dreams | Writing strong concluding remarks in a persuasive speech | Give a speech in which you encourage your classmates to make a change in their lives |

# Childhood Memories

## Warm-up

Read about each person's childhood memory. Then tell the class which memory you think is the best.

When I was seven years old, my parents took my sister and me to a Cirque du Soleil show. It's my happiest childhood memory.

One of my best childhood memories is when my sister and I visited my grandmother in Malaysia. My grandmother cooked really delicious food and my sister and I played in the ocean every day.

When I was five years old, I met Lionel Messi at an autograph signing. He signed my poster and my soccer ball. I couldn't even say hello to him because I was so nervous.

When I was eleven years old, I had my tonsils removed. It was painful, and I had to stay in the hospital. However, I didn't have to go to school, and the nurses let me eat ice cream every day!

**Childhood Memories** When giving a speech about a childhood memory, you can use descriptive language to tell the audience how you felt. This will make your story less repetitive and more interesting. You should also use the past tense to indicate when the event took place.

## Vocabulary

A  Read about childhood memories and then circle the correct words.

1  I remember going on a field trip to a local farm when I was in the first grade. The experience was (remarkable / mind numbing). It inspired me to study agriculture at university.

2  Losing my teeth when I was very young made me happy because I received a silver dollar from the tooth fairy each time I lost a tooth. Of course, it was my father who actually gave me the money. I recently saw a picture of myself from that time period. I looked so (silly / serious) with a big gap in my smile.

3  My family took a road trip across the United States in an RV when I was twelve. We visited the Grand Canyon. The (picturesque / dull) canyon was remarkable. It was a view I will never forget.

4  Some of my favorite memories from childhood are the sleepovers my friends and I used to have. We would tell ghost stories to one another. My friend Beth was really good at telling (ridiculous / frightening) stories. Her stories terrified us so much that we couldn't sleep.

5  When I was in the sixth grade, I was in a school musical. My knees were shaking throughout the entire performance. It was (a nerve-racking / an unmemorable) experience. I never volunteered to be in a school performance again.

B  **Pair work | Ask your partner to share a happy childhood memory with you.**

## Grammar

A  Let's learn about regular and irregular past simple tense verbs.

| Regular Past Simple Tense Verbs | | Irregular Past Simple Tense Verbs | |
|---|---|---|---|
| visit – visit**ed** | decide – decid**ed** | see – **saw** | eat – **ate** |
| enjoy – enjoy**ed** | watch – watch**ed** | go – **went** | drive – **drove** |
| stop – stop**ped** | travel – travel**ed** | ride – **rode** | buy – **bought** |

*All regular past simple tense verbs end in *-ed*. Irregular past simple tense verbs do not follow a standard set of rules. Their past tense forms must be memorized.

B  Complete the sentences by using the correct forms of the verbs in the past simple tense.

1  Erica's family _____ to China. (move)

2  We _____ the Grand Canyon last year. (see)

3  My family _____ horses in Hawaii. (ride)

4  They _____ to visit the Louvre. (want)

5  Jin _____ a souvenir in Thailand. (buy)

6  Our flight _____ in Singapore. (stop)

**The Beginning, Middle, and Ending** A speech about a childhood memory requires the speaker to be a good storyteller. A good story requires a beginning, a middle, and an ending. There are a number of sequence words that one can use in order to tell the beginning, middle, and ending of a story.

## Language Patterns

A Read the examples of sequence words and expressions.

| Beginning of the Story | Middle of the Story | Ending of the Story |
|---|---|---|
| First of all | Then | Eventually |
| To begin with | After that | Ultimately |
| To start with | Later | At last |

B **Speaking** | Tell brief stories about lifetime firsts. Remember to include a beginning, a middle, and an ending to your stories.

> When I was ten, my mother burst into my room at 6:00 a.m. and shrieked, "You have to get up!" My parents had planned a surprise trip to Universal Studios in Los Angeles, California. To begin with, we flew in an airplane, which was exciting because it was my first time. After that, we checked into a hotel which had a pool. I loved that. Eventually, we made it to Universal Studios. Unfortunately, we had to spend most of the day waiting in lines for rides because there were so many people!

## Pronunciation 🔊

A Read and listen to the sentences below. Then practice the common reductions of *had to* and *have to*.

| when written | when spoken |
|---|---|
| We **had to** arrive at the airport early. | We ***hadta*** arrive at the airport early. |
| Sujin doesn't **have to** check any luggage. | Sujin doesn't ***hafta*** check any luggage. |

B Listen and practice. Be careful when pronouncing *had to* and *have to*.

1 Jin **had to** warm up before the performance.

2 Annie and James **have to** check in now.

3 When I was thirteen, my parents told me I **had to** go to ballet camp.

4 I **have to** tell you a story. It's about how I wound up living in France.

**Details in the Story**  In a speech about a childhood memory, you should include the details that made the experience memorable. Your recollection of the events that occurred and the emotions that you felt at the time will help create an interesting narrative for the audience to enjoy.

# Reading 🔊

Read about each person's childhood memory.

When I was eleven, my parents took my family to Niagara Falls in New York. My family lives in Massachusetts, so we had to drive for several hours to get there. My brother and I wanted to go to Disney World, but my mom and dad really wanted to see the falls. I remember my father getting angry with my brother and me because we fought a lot in the car. Seeing the falls was cool, but after half an hour, my brother and I were bored. We stayed there for three days. I don't remember much about the trip, but I know it wasn't that much fun.

- Dustin

My dog Rufus died when I was five years old. It was devastating. He was thirteen years old, so he had had a long life for a dog, but I was too young to understand that. I remember crying and hugging my mother's leg because I missed Rufus so much. About three months later, my mother and father bought a new dog, Buddy. He was a golden retriever, too. Buddy lived for fifteen years and died when I was 21 years old. His death was even more painful because I knew Buddy for his entire life.

- Lina

When I was in junior high school, my friends used to sleep over at my house on weekends. We would order pizza and watch scary movies all night. My house had a living room in the basement, where we could watch movies and sleep without being disturbed. Those memories are some of the best memories in my life. We didn't have to worry about anything except school. Now that all of us have jobs, we talk about all of the good times we used to have together in junior high school.

- Sarah

**Following the Reading**   Answer the questions.

1  Where did Dustin's family go on a trip?

2  What did Dustin think about the trip?

3  How old was Rufus when he died?

4  Why was Buddy's death more painful for Lina?

5  What did Sarah and her friend do during sleepovers?

6  What do Sarah and her friends talk about when they get together these days?

# Learning How

**Brainstorming** Begin the speechwriting process by doing a brainstorming session. Brainstorming helps ideas and memories flow out in an uninterrupted way. Once you have exhausted your memories of the event, you should keep the most important details and dispose of the rest. Below are three examples of useful brainstorming strategies.

A  Look at the three different examples of brainstorming strategies for the same speech topic. Then complete the missing information in each section by referring to strategies from the other sections.

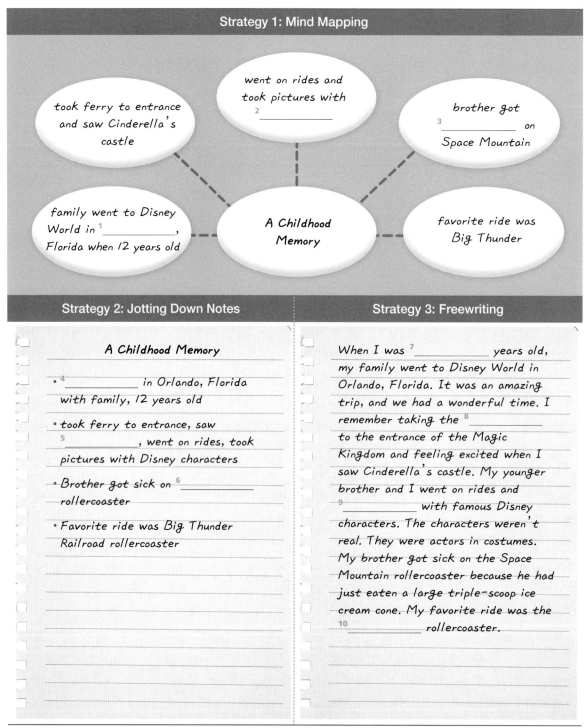

**Strategy 1: Mind Mapping**

took ferry to entrance and saw Cinderella's castle

went on rides and took pictures with 2 _____

brother got 3 _____ on Space Mountain

family went to Disney World in 1 _____, Florida when 12 years old

A Childhood Memory

favorite ride was Big Thunder

**Strategy 2: Jotting Down Notes**

A Childhood Memory

• 4 _____ in Orlando, Florida with family, 12 years old

• took ferry to entrance, saw 5 _____, went on rides, took pictures with Disney characters

• Brother got sick on 6 _____ rollercoaster

• Favorite ride was Big Thunder Railroad rollercoaster

**Strategy 3: Freewriting**

When I was 7 _____ years old, my family went to Disney World in Orlando, Florida. It was an amazing trip, and we had a wonderful time. I remember taking the 8 _____ to the entrance of the Magic Kingdom and feeling excited when I saw Cinderella's castle. My younger brother and I went on rides and 9 _____ with famous Disney characters. The characters weren't real. They were actors in costumes. My brother got sick on the Space Mountain rollercoaster because he had just eaten a large triple-scoop ice cream cone. My favorite ride was the 10 _____ rollercoaster.

B   Imagine you went on a field trip to a museum when you were in elementary school. Complete one of the strategies by using the field trip itinerary below.

| Museum Field Trip Itinerary | |
|---|---|
| **9:45 a.m.** | students board the bus in front of the school |
| **10:30 a.m.** | arrive at the museum / tour guide gives students a tour of the museum |
| **Noon** | have lunch |
| **1:15 p.m.** | students visit the museum gift shop |
| **2:30 p.m.** | students board the bus in front of the museum |
| **3:00 p.m.** | students return to the school |

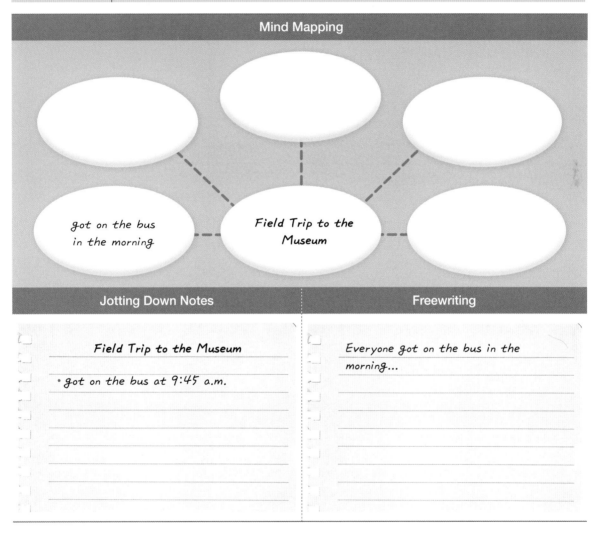

**Mind Mapping**

got on the bus in the morning

Field Trip to the Museum

**Jotting Down Notes**

*Field Trip to the Museum*

• got on the bus at 9:45 a.m.

**Freewriting**

*Everyone got on the bus in the morning...*

🗸 **Common Mistakes** **homonyms and homophones**

board (noun): a wooden plank          board (verb): to get on a bus, airplane, or train

bored: a lack of interest in an activity or situation

# Do It Yourself

**The Narrative Speech: A Childhood Memory** Now it is time for you to do it yourself! Use the information you learned in the previous sections in order to create an outline for a speech telling a story about a childhood memory.

A Do brainstorming sessions for the topic "A Childhood Memory" by using one of the strategies below.

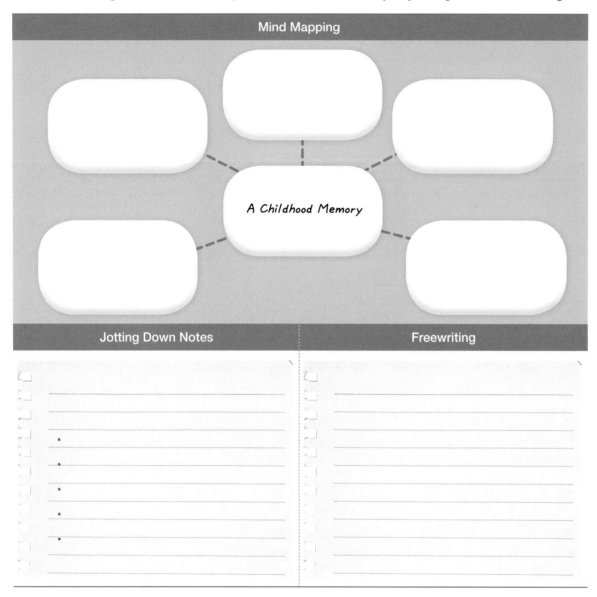

B Write down the most important details from your brainstorming sessions in the space below.

C Give a short speech about a childhood memory. Use your notes from B. Don't forget to use the sequence words and expressions.

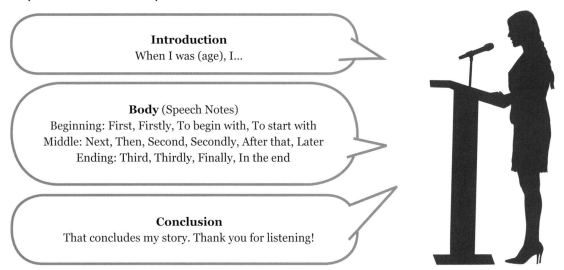

**Introduction**
When I was (age), I…

**Body** (Speech Notes)
Beginning: First, Firstly, To begin with, To start with
Middle: Next, Then, Second, Secondly, After that, Later
Ending: Third, Thirdly, Finally, In the end

**Conclusion**
That concludes my story. Thank you for listening!

# Checklist

1 What can descriptive language tell the audience?
2 What does every good story require?
3 What two factors will help create an interesting narrative for the audience to enjoy?
4 What should the first step in the speech-writing process be?
5 What three brainstorming strategies are mentioned in the unit?

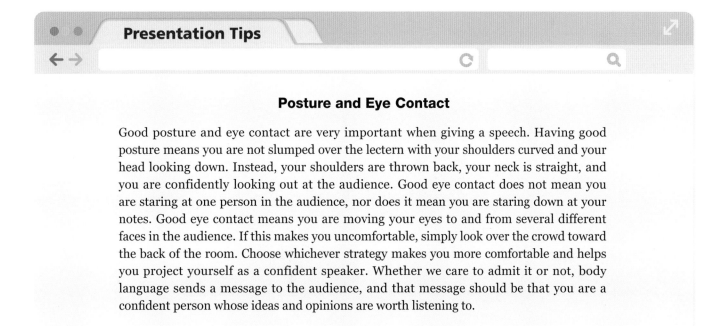

**Presentation Tips**

## Posture and Eye Contact

Good posture and eye contact are very important when giving a speech. Having good posture means you are not slumped over the lectern with your shoulders curved and your head looking down. Instead, your shoulders are thrown back, your neck is straight, and you are confidently looking out at the audience. Good eye contact does not mean you are staring at one person in the audience, nor does it mean you are staring down at your notes. Good eye contact means you are moving your eyes to and from several different faces in the audience. If this makes you uncomfortable, simply look over the crowd toward the back of the room. Choose whichever strategy makes you more comfortable and helps you project yourself as a confident speaker. Whether we care to admit it or not, body language sends a message to the audience, and that message should be that you are a confident person whose ideas and opinions are worth listening to.

# Success

## Warm-up

Look at the pictures and brief descriptions. Check all the boxes that you think represent success.

**1** Accomplishing something physically demanding ☐

**2** Earning a lot of money ☐

**3** Having a loving family ☐

**4** Getting a promotion at work ☐

**5** Finding a romantic partner ☐

**6** Getting a degree ☐

**Words Related to Success** When giving a definitional speech about success, vocabulary that is specifically related to the idea of success can be very helpful. By using more precise language surrounding a topic, the speech becomes more interesting and coherent for an audience.

## Vocabulary

A Match the words with the correct definitions.

| | | | |
|---|---|---|---|
| 1 attitude | • | • a | hard work; energy used to accomplish something |
| 2 character | • | • b | ultimate success; the highest achievement |
| 3 effort | • | • c | a person's moral quality |
| 4 perseverance | • | • d | a person's way of thinking |
| 5 prosperousness | • | • e | personal wealth; success; riches |
| 6 victory | • | • f | not giving up; trying to accomplish something despite its difficulty |

B **Pair work** | **Ask your partner about a personal victory he or she is proud of.**

A I am proud of getting my bachelor of science degree at my university. It took a lot of effort, but I graduated.

B I think you're going to have a great career now. Perseverance is an excellent predictor of success.

## Grammar

A **Let's learn about gerunds and infinitives.**

| Gerund (verb + -ing) | Infinitive (to + verb) |
|---|---|
| Gerunds can be used after these verbs: *enjoy, like, dislike, finish, avoid, mind.* | Infinitives can be used after these verbs: *agree, decide, help, hope, learn, promise, plan, want, would like.* |
| Do you mind **spending** your weekends at home instead of on the golf course? | Alan decided **to help** Janet achieve her goal of becoming a CEO. |
| Gerunds should be used when following prepositions such as *before, by, of, in,* and *after.* | Infinitives can be used after some adjectives. |
| Exercise before **going** to work. You'll feel better. | We are excited **to learn** more about the business venture. |
| Gerunds can be used as subjects or objects in sentences. | Infinitives can be used as subjects or objects; however, they are not normally used as subjects. |
| **Sacrificing** your free time to help a friend is a good character trait. | Jin likes **to walk** in the evenings. |

B **Complete each sentence by using the correct gerund or infinitive.**

1 Angie is excited _____ on the presentation with her team members. (work)

2 Jin and Chao decided _____ on the project. (collaborate)

3 Teamwork can be achieved by _____ together to work toward a common goal. (come)

4 _____ during a difficult time shows character. (persevere)

5 I promise _____ realistic goals and to work hard to achieve them. (set)

**Defining Terms in a Speech**  When giving a definitional speech, it is important to learn some expressions commonly used to define terms in the speech. Defining terms clearly for an audience is important because it reduces confusion and misunderstandings. The audience knows what you mean by these terms.

# Language Patterns

A  Read and practice the expressions used to define terms.

| Defining Terms in a Speech | | |
| --- | --- | --- |
| My idea of ~ is...<br>I believe ~ is... | My definition of ~ is...<br>I think ~ can be defined as... | I define ~ as...<br>~ is... |

B  Match the expressions with the correct pictures. Then define them in your own words by using the expressions in A.

| | | |
| --- | --- | --- |
| a.  a successful home life | b.  a successful business meeting | c.  a successful friendship |
| d.  a successful career | e.  successful teamwork | f.  a successful romance |

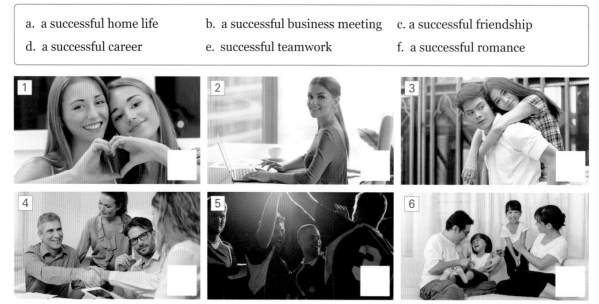

*I define a successful home life as having a loving spouse and two beautiful children. My idea of a successful career is having a job that pays very well...*

# Pronunciation 🔊

A  Read and listen to the sentences below. Then practice the common reductions of *of a* and *of an*.

| of a = "uva" | of an = "uvan" |
| --- | --- |
| What's your definition **of a** successful business strategy? | My definition **of an** unsuccessful business strategy is one that lacks long-term planning. |

B  Listen and practice. Be careful when pronouncing these common reductions.

A What's your definition **of a** successful education?

B My definition **of a** successful education is one that helps a student grow intellectually and morally but also provides that person with useful career skills. What's your idea **of an** unsuccessful education?

A My definition **of an** unsuccessful education is one that doesn't prepare a person for life.

**Subtopics Related to Success**  When giving a speech defining what success means to you, you can talk about a variety of subtopics. You might want to talk about how you define career success or a successful home life. As the speaker, you can outline the parameters of the speech as you see fit.

# Reading 🔊

Read about each person's idea of success.

Achieving professional success is very important to me. I want to work hard while I am young so that I can be successful later. I believe success can be defined as having a position of authority at a large multinational company. I want to be one of the employees at the company who makes decisions regarding the future of the company. I want to be a leader. I define leadership as being a member of a group who is respected by his or her peers, someone who people listen to, and someone who isn't afraid to make tough decisions.

- Tom

My definition of success is having a happy home life and a healthy family. My six-year-old daughter Emma is the most important part of my life. I quit working when I got pregnant. Professional success is not important to me. I define success as being a great mother and raising a happy and healthy child. Money is sometimes tight in our family because we are a single-income family. But there are more important things in life than money.

- Esther

I think good health can be defined as having a healthy body as well as a peaceful mind. We often forget about good mental health when considering the status of our overall health. It is easy to get caught up in the rat race of everyday life. Every morning, I do yoga in order to keep my body healthy, and I meditate for 20 minutes in order to make my mind calm. Meditation relaxes me and reduces my overall anxiety. This, in turn, prepares me for the many challenges I may face throughout the day and allows me to handle them more effectively and healthfully.

- Janine

**Following the Reading**   Change the incorrect statements into correct statements.

1  Tom believes a leader is someone who isn't afraid to let the group make tough decisions.

2  Esther quit working when her daughter turned six years old.

3  Janine defines good health as having a perfect body and an anxious mind.

4  Janine does yoga for 20 minutes every morning.

## Learning How

**Transitions** Transitions separate the body of the speech into manageable pieces. They tell the audience that you are moving from the introduction to main point 1, from main point 1 to main point 2, and so on. Most speeches contain three main points; however, greater or fewer than that is possible.

A **Read the body of Anna's speech. Then insert the transitions below into the correct places in the speech.**

| | |
|---|---|
| a | I have defined a successful career. Now, let me talk about what I believe a successful home life is. |
| b | I have told you about my idea of a successful home life. Now, let me summarize today's talk. |
| c | To begin, let me talk about my definition of a successful relationship. |
| d | I have talked about my idea of a successful relationship. Now, let me talk about how I define a successful career. |

**1**

My idea of a successful relationship is being with a guy who really loves me and treats me well. I would like to date a man who has professional goals like me. I also want someone who is kind, gentle, protective, and loyal. Those are very important qualities in a partner. **2** My definition of a successful career is achieving a leadership role at my company. I don't want to simply follow someone else's instructions. Instead, I want to be one of the people at the company making important decisions and leading a group of workers. I believe I have a lot to offer a company in terms of good ideas. I want people **3** to listen to me and, of course, to pay me well for those ideas. My definition of a successful home life is being married to the kind of man I have already described earlier in the speech. I also want to have one or two happy and healthy children with this man. I want a career, too, so my husband and I will share equally in the responsibilities associated with raising a family and taking care of a home. We will be a busy family, but it will be a loving home! **4**

B   Read the body of Simon's speech. Then write transitions that would help him move from one section of the speech to another.

Being the owner of a successful bakery hasn't been easy. It took a lot of hard work to get here. There are three aspects of success that I would like to talk to you about today. First, I want to define successful leadership for you. Then, I would like to tell you what my idea of teamwork is. Finally, I want to tell you what I believe a successful career is. (Transition 1) *To start with, I'd like to...*

I think successful leadership is leading by example. In the beginning, I could only afford to pay one other employee. That meant that the two of us had to divvy up the entire workload. Some bosses might have given their employee all of the dirty work, such as taking out the garbage and cleaning the dishes. But I decided not to do that. We both did these jobs, and I think that it made a difference. I was able to earn my employee's respect because I didn't think I was too important to get my hands dirty, too. (Transition 2)

My definition of successful teamwork is when every member of the team has respect for the other members. When my bakery became more successful, I hired two more workers. I made sure that the people I hired had good attitudes and treated each other well. Most importantly, I made sure that I also treated my employees with dignity and respect. By showing my workers that I could also be a generous and cooperative team member, it inspired them to do the same. (Transition 3)

Career success is not about money for me. I like that my bakery is doing well financially and that I now employ more than ten people at two different locations; however, knowing that my staff members like me and respect me as a leader is more important than money. I think that is why so many of my employees have stayed with me over the past ten years. (Transition 4)

💬 **Common Mistakes  a loving home vs. a lovely home**

a loving home = a home with a family who cares for and loves one another

a lovely home = a nicely built house with a well-decorated interior and exterior

## Do It Yourself

**The Informative Speech: How Do You Define Success?** Now it is time for you to do it yourself! Use the information you learned in the previous sections in order to create an outline for a speech describing how you define success.

A In the empty space provided, use one of the brainstorming strategies discussed in Unit 1. Then create an outline for the speech in the space below.

| Brainstorming | | |
| --- | --- | --- |
| ☐ mind-mapping | ☐ jotting down notes | ☐ freewriting |

| Body |
| --- |

Transition 1:

Main Point 1:

Transition 2:

Main Point 2:

Transition 3:

Main Point 3:

Transition 4:

B  Give a short speech about your definition of success. Use your notes from A. Don't forget to use transitions in the speech.

**Introduction and Preview of Main Points**
Today, I would like to tell you how I define success. I will tell you what my definition of a successful friendship is, what a successful home life is, and what my idea of a successful career is.

**Body** (Speech Notes)
To start with, let me talk about what my definition of a successful friendship is.

**Summary and Concluding Remarks**
Today, I talked about my definitions of a successful friendship, home life, and career. Thank you for listening to my talk.

# Checklist

1  Why is it helpful to use precise language when discussing a topic?
2  Why should we define terms clearly for an audience?
3  What purpose do transitions serve?
4  What do transitions communicate to an audience?

## Presentation Tips

### Volume of Voice and Using a Lectern

When giving a speech, it is very important that everyone in the audience can hear you. If your voice is not loud enough for the audience members sitting in the back row to hear you, use a microphone. If the back row can hear you, don't use a microphone. It is important to project your voice with confidence, and it does not hurt to have a bottle of water near you in case you get a quick bout of dry mouth. Do not chew gum during your speech as this can prove distracting to an audience and also makes people believe that you are not taking the speech very seriously. You may choose to stand behind the lectern or to pace slowly back and forth across the stage. Both forms are acceptable; however, the use of a lectern gives you the opportunity to rest your notes on it. Never lean or rest on the lectern. This portrays an image or weakness or nervousness.

# How to Do Something

## Warm-up

Write the speech topics under the correct pictures.

| | | |
|---|---|---|
| How to build a campfire | How to buy a used car | How to set up an aquarium |
| How to make a salad | How to use a fire extinguisher | How to write a résumé |

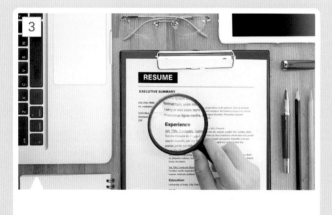

**Using Nuanced Language** When giving a "How to" speech, it is important to use nuanced language so that the listener knows the action is advised, necessary, possible, or prohibited. We achieve nuance by using modal auxiliary verbs in English. There are several examples of them below.

## Vocabulary

Complete the sentences with the correct words from the word box.

| used | résumés | fire extinguisher | survival | set up | healthfully |
|---|---|---|---|---|---|

1 Today, I would like to teach you how to build a campfire. This basic _____ skill is something everyone should know how to do.

2 If you are thinking about buying a bike, you might want to consider buying a _____ one.

3 You never know when a fire might break out. Today, I'm going to teach you how to properly use a _____.

4 If you are looking for a good hobby, setting up a fish aquarium might be a fun and rewarding one for you. Today, I'm going to show you how to _____ an aquarium in your house.

5 College graduates must learn to write good _____ so that they can get their dream jobs.

6 You must eat _____ if you want to have a fit body and a healthy heart. So today I'm going to teach you how to make a delicious and healthy salad.

## Grammar

A Let's learn about modal auxiliary verbs.

| Might<br>We use *might* if we want to express possibility. | Must<br>We use *must* if we want to express obligation. | Should<br>We use *should* when we are giving advice. |
|---|---|---|
| Joining a gym **might** be fun and good for you.<br>This file type **might not** work with your device. | You **must** choose a serious font for your résumé.<br>People with heart disease **must not** use this medicine. | You **should** learn some basic survival techniques.<br>You **should** learn some good basic study habits before attending university. |

B Complete the sentences with the correct modal auxiliary verbs.

1 You _____ bring a first-aid kid on a camping trip. Not doing so is very irresponsible.

2 You _____ learn how to play a musical instrument because it can enrich your life.

3 For public safety, restaurant owners _____ teach their servers the Heimlich maneuver. If they don't, they should have to pay a fine to the government.

4 If you don't like working out in a gym, you _____ enjoy hiking for exercise.

5 We _____ make an effort to really listen to others when they speak. It improves the quality of communication between individuals and reduces misunderstandings.

**The Sequence of Events** When giving a "How to" speech, it is important to use sequence words so that the audience knows in which order the actions should occur. Sequence words give the audience a better understanding of the process being described.

# Language Patterns

A Read and practice the sequence words.

| Sequence Words | | | | |
|---|---|---|---|---|
| First | Second | Third | Fourth | Finally |
| Firstly | Secondly | Thirdly | Fourthly | Last |
| First up | Second of all | Third of all | Fourth of all | Lastly |
| First of all | Next | | | Last of all |
| | Next up | | | |

B Look at the picture cues and describe the steps needed to change a flat tire. Use the sequence words in A to complete your description.

1 TURN ON THE HAZARD LIGHTS

2 SET THE PARKING BRAKE & BLOCKING THE WHEEL

3 REMOVE THE HUB CAP

4 JACK THE CAR UP & CHANGE THE WHEEL

*First of all, you must turn on the hazard lights. Next...*

# Pronunciation 🔊

A Read and listen to the words below. Then practice the pronunciations of the /z/ and /dʒ/ sounds.

| /z/ | | /dʒ/ | |
|---|---|---|---|
| hazard | opens | jack | just |
| turns | résumé | change | wedge |

B Listen and practice. Be careful when pronouncing the /z/ and /dʒ/ sounds.

1 Changing the tire on a car is a difficult process.

2 Wedge the screwdriver between the boards.

3 Wear protective goggles just in case there is an accident.

**The Steps in a Process** When giving a "How to" speech, it is important to introduce the topic briefly in a few sentences. This lets the audience know what is being discussed. Then, each step should be clearly explained so that the audience can visualize the process being described.

# Reading 🔊

**Read about how to do each activity.**

One of the most important aspects of outdoor survival is the ability to build a shelter. I'd like to tell you how to build a proper shelter. First of all, you need to find the right area to build your shelter in. It must be on high ground in order to prevent flooding from rain or high tides. If you can, you should find an area that is already protected by rocks, trees, or other vegetation. Second of all, you need to build a basic structure. This can be done by using thick tree branches or small tree trunks. Drive two sticks vertically into the ground. Next, connect them by tying a horizontally placed branch between them. Last of all, lay as many long branches as you can find against the horizontally placed branch. This will create a slope that will direct any rainfall away from the center of the shelter. You may also place leaves, mud, and brush in the cracks of the roof in order to make the shelter more rain and wind resistant. This is how you build a shelter in the woods.

- James

When I was eleven years old, I witnessed a man choke on a piece of steak in a restaurant. Everybody in the restaurant froze except for a woman near the back of restaurant. The woman promptly performed the Heimlich maneuver on the man, saving his life. It was then that I decided I too wanted to learn the Heimlich maneuver, so I could possibly save someone's life in the future. I'd like to teach you the Heimlich maneuver right now. First of all, you need to stand behind the choking person with one foot placed back slightly for balance. Next up, make a fist and place it just above the person's bellybutton. After that, grasp your fist with the  other hand and thrust upward into the person's abdomen. Lastly, perform six to ten thrusts until the piece of food is dislodged from the person's throat. This is how you perform the Heimlich maneuver.

- Sue

**Following the Reading**   **Answer the questions.**

1  What is one of the most important aspects of outdoor survival?

2  Why should you build your shelter on high ground?

3  Why do you want to place leaves, mud, and brush in the cracks of the roof?

4  What happened to Sue when she was eleven years old?

5  When performing the Heimlich maneuver, why should you place one foot back slightly?

6  Where should you place your hands when performing the Heimlich maneuver?

**Attention-Getting Opener Strategies**  The hook comes at the beginning of the introduction and helps you grab the audience's attention in an interesting way. There are multiple strategies you can use in order to grab an audience's attention. The following are some of the most common strategies speakers use.

A  Match the attention-getting opener strategies to the correct examples.

> a  State a shocking fact or statistic related to the topic of your speech.
>
> b  Ask the audience a rhetorical question, a question that does not require a response and that serves only a stylistic purpose.
>
> c  Use an anecdote or a short story in order to grab the audience's attention.
>
> d  Use a relevant quotation from a famous person.
>
> e  Use a visual aid such as a picture, a video, or an object.
>
> f  Use a gimmick such as a short performance or audience participation in order to get the attention of the audience.

(1) When I was nine, my father took me on a weeklong camping trip. The experience sparked my interest in the outdoors and inspired me to become an outdoor survivalist.

(2) This picture shows the universal sign for choking.

(3) Have you ever bought a used car? If so, were you worried that the car you just bought was a lemon?

(4) David Beckham said, "I don't have time for hobbies. At the end of the day, I treat my job as a hobby. It's something I love doing."

(5) Everybody, please take a cup and a fork. Inside the cup is a sample of my famous salmon and walnut salad. Today, I'm going to show you how to make it yourselves!

(6) 60% of Americans say they cannot change a flat tire on their car.

*lemon: a slang word for a used car that breaks down very soon after being purchased

B   Complete the "How to" topics with your own choice of topics. After that, write attention-getting openers in the spaces provided. Finally, take turns delivering your openers to a partner.

| ex. | Shocking Statistic |

Topic: How to **buy** *a used car*

39.2 million used cars were sold in the United States in 2017.

| 1 | Rhetorical Question |

Topic: How to **go**...

| 2 | Anecdote |

Topic: How to **cook**...

| 3 | Famous Quote |

Topic: How to **raise**...

| 4 | Photograph or Picture (You can show the image on your smartphone.) |

Topic: How to **wash**...

| 5 | Gimmick |

Topic: How to **do**...

---

🎯 **Common Mistakes  vertically vs. horizontally**

vertically = up and down          horizontally = across / left and right

# Do It Yourself

**The Informative Speech: How to Do Something** Now it is time for you to do it yourself! Use the information you learned in the previous sections in order to create an outline for a speech explaining how to do something.

A Brainstorm an outline for the speech and choose an attention-getting opener strategy in order to write your opener. Then create a body and conclusion for the speech.

| Brainstorming |
| --- |

| Attention-Getting Opener |
| --- |

Which strategy would you choose for your attention-getting opener?
- ☐ shocking statistic
- ☐ famous quote
- ☐ rhetorical question
- ☐ visual aid
- ☐ anecdote
- ☐ gimmick

Now, write your attention-getting opener.

| Body |
| --- |

Transition 1:

Main Point 1 (Step 1):

Transition 2:

Main Point 2 (Step 2):

Transition 3:

Main Point 3 (Step 3):

Transition 4:

| Summary and Concluding Remarks |
| --- |

B Give a short speech about how to do something. Use your notes from A. Don't forget to use ordinal numbers and sequence adverbs to describe the steps in the process.

# Checklist

1 Why is it important to use nuanced language in a "How to" speech?
2 Why is it important to use sequence words in a speech?
3 What is the purpose of a hook?
4 Name six attention-getting opener strategies discussed in the unit.

**Presentation Tips**

## The Extemporaneous Delivery

When delivering a speech, the best method of delivery is the extemporaneous delivery. Speaking extemporaneously does not mean you have memorized the speech, nor does it mean you are reading the speech from a piece of paper or a teleprompter. Speaking extemporaneously means you remember the major details you wish to convey to the audience and deliver them in a conversational way that feels authentic or genuine. When speaking in this manner, it is okay to occasionally glance at your notes, where you have written down some key words, phrases, or quotations. It is not okay to spend the majority of the speech reading from your notes. Your notes should serve the purpose of jogging your memory so that you can maintain good eye contact with the audience as you deliver the speech in a conversational manner.

# Locations around the World



## Warm-up

**Look at the map and fill in each blank with the correct country's name.**

| | | |
|---|---|---|
| Canada | South Korea | China |
| Italy | Brazil | India |

1
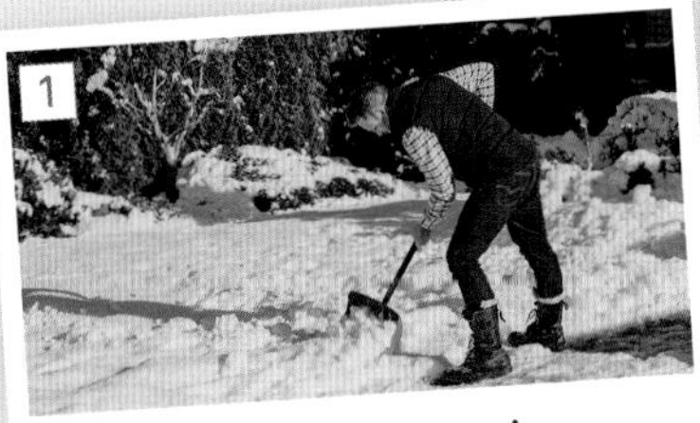
Shoveling snow in ________

2
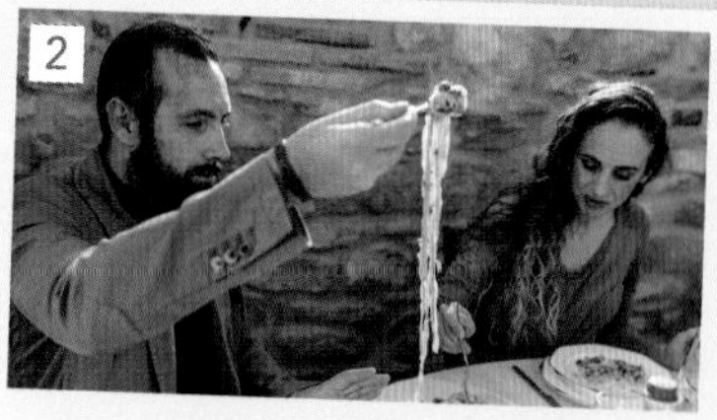
Eating pasta in ________

3
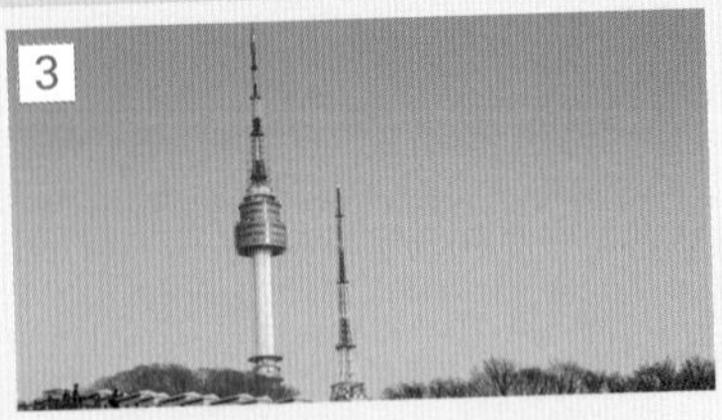
Visiting N. Seoul Tower in ________

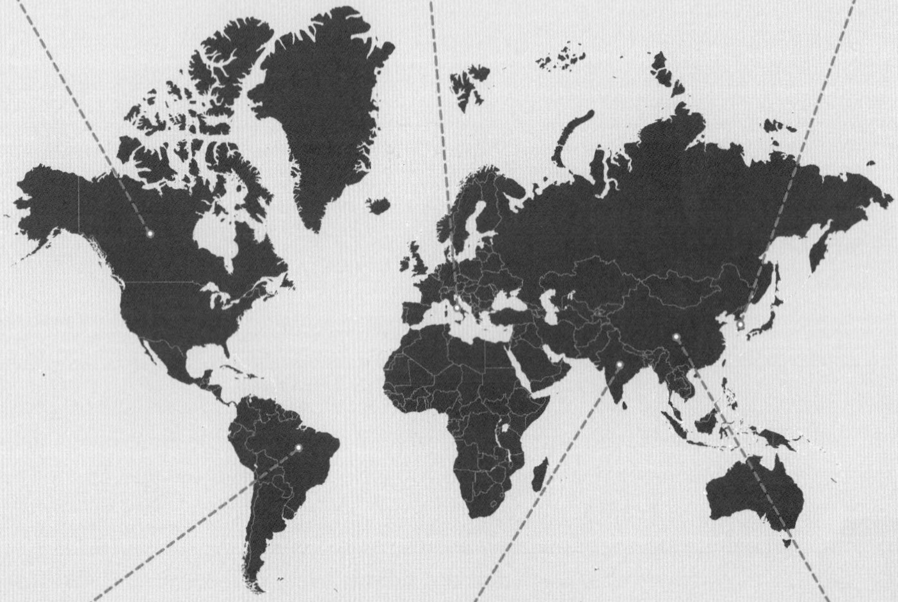

4
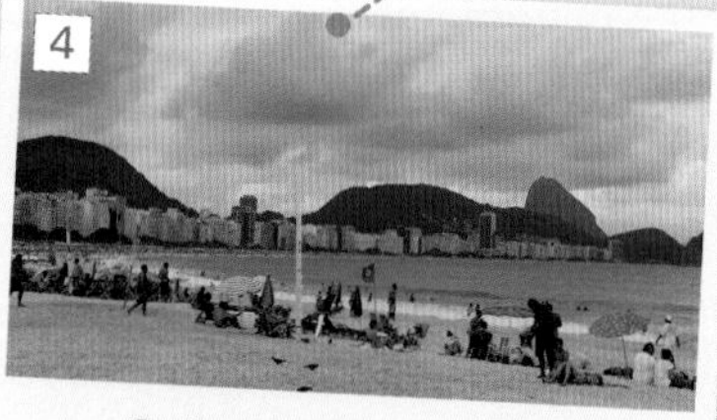
Going to the beach in ________

5
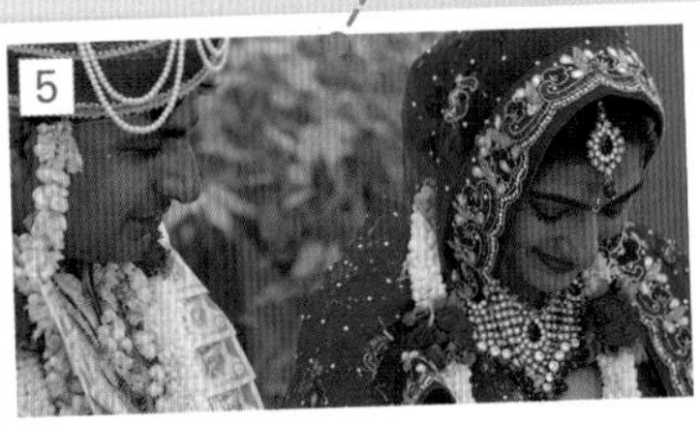
Getting married in ________

6
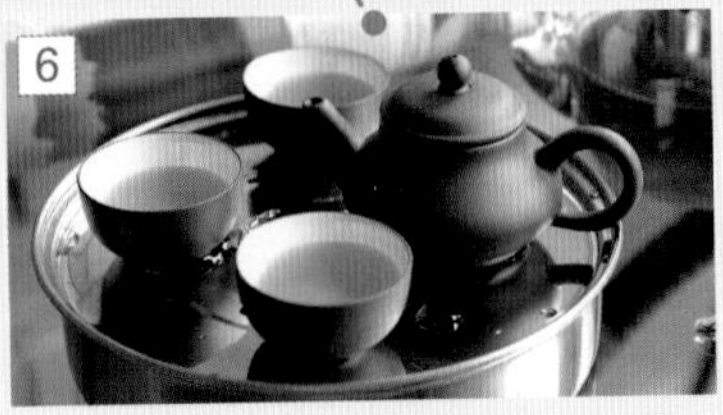
Drinking tea in ________

**Perceptions** When giving a speech about one topic and how it is perceived in different parts of the world, it is a good idea to think about how countries differ. For example, what are the geography and the climate like? What is the government like? This will help you narrow down your topic.

## Vocabulary

A  Complete the sentences with the correct words from the word box.

| wedding ceremony | coastline | skyline | blizzard | nightlife | urban |
|---|---|---|---|---|---|

1  Hong Kong is famous for its great shopping, interesting cuisine, and wild _____.

2  Brazil's beautiful _____ has a number of world-famous beaches.

3  Canadians hate shoveling their walkways the morning after a big _____.

4  Shanghai is one of the most vibrant _____ centers in the world.

5  The sparkling gold-colored 63 Building is prominently featured in Seoul's _____.

6  A _____ in India is quite different than one in Saudi Arabia.

B  **Pair work** | Interview your partner about wedding ceremonies in his or her country.

| Tell me about _____ in your country. | |
|---|---|
| wedding ceremonies | |
| wedding garments | |
| wedding meals | |

A  Women often wear *hanboks*, traditional Korean garments, to weddings in my country.
B  That's really interesting. What do they look like?
A  They're beautiful and they come in many different colors.

## Grammar

A  Let's learn about prepositions of place.

| alongside, along, among, against, around |
|---|

Let's take a walk **alongside** the river.
Driving **along** the winding roads of San Francisco can be scary.
**Among** African countries, Nigeria is the richest.
The majority of Europeans are **against** the death penalty.
Apartments in and **around** urban centers are expensive in most cities.

B  Complete the sentences by using the prepositions in A.

1  Property in and _____ downtown Seoul is very expensive.

2  Residents of British Columbia enjoy taking walks _____ the streams and rivers there.

3  Shanghai is _____ the most populated and modern cities in the world.

4  Driving _____ the Pacific Coast Highway is a popular weekend activity in California.

5  Many Japanese are _____ the use of coal to meet the country's energy needs.

**Differences** When giving a speech about different parts of the world, it is helpful to use language that can provide a contrast between different locations. The differences between two locations give the audience a clearer understanding of each place.

# Language Patterns

A Read and practice the expressions for stating opposite ideas.

> **yet, however, conversely, on the other hand, on the contrary**

The European Union has its own currency, **yet** the U.K. still uses the pound.
Hawaii is a beautiful vacation spot; **however**, Thailand is cheaper and just as beautiful.
The U.S. economy is quite robust. **Conversely**, the markets in Japan aren't doing well.
The transportation systems in Asian countries are excellent. **On the other hand**, the North American transportation system is crumbling.
Americans prefer milk chocolate. **On the contrary**, Australians have a preference for dark chocolate.

B Choose a topic and two locations. Then think of ways in which your topic is different in each location. State the differences by using the expressions in A.

> Finding a restaurant in the United States that serves an authentic English breakfast is easy; however, finding a restaurant in Japan that serves a real English breakfast is much more difficult.

# Pronunciation 🔊

A Read and listen to the sentences below. Then practice the common reduction of the /d/ and /j/ sounds.

> **ending sound /d/ + beginning sound /j/ = /dʒ/ sound**

What similarities do you an**d y**our brother share?
Are you an**d y**our mother tall?
Are your country an**d y**our neighboring country similar?
Why'**d y**ou visit Australia last year?

B Listen and practice. Be careful when pronouncing the ending sound /d/ with the beginning sound /j/.

1 Which vineyard di**d y**ou visit in Italy?

2 What are you an**d y**our friend going to do in Europe this summer?

3 Di**d y**ou know the climate in Tennessee is similar to the climate in South Korea?

4 Are you an**d y**our sister coming to the party on Friday?

5 Why'**d y**ou decide to visit the Philippines again this winter?

**Different Locations** Although it is not a rule, it is common for speechwriters to include three main points in the body of a speech. When giving a speech with a location organizational pattern, you can talk about one topic and how it applies in three different locations in the world.

## Reading 🔊

Read about each topic and the different locations.

I'd like to tell you about family dynamics in three different regions of the world: North America, Asia, and the Middle East. North Americans are generally more independent and individualistic. They are taught the importance of self-responsibility from an early age. Although their parents may disagree with their decisions, such as what kind of career to pursue or whom to marry, they will ultimately follow their own instincts. In Asia, the family dynamic is more interconnected. Children are often seen as an extension of their parents, and thus a child's behavior has a powerful impact on the parents' public reputations. Decisions such as career and marriage are strongly influenced by the parents and even the grandparents. In the Middle East, decisions such as career and marriage are quite heavily influenced by immediate and extended family members. Cultivating strong relationships with relatives is very important. These family bonds are often strengthened through customs and festivals.

I want to talk to you about the subway systems in New York City, Seoul, and Tokyo. Although New York City has a vast subway system, it can be quite intimidating to an outsider. Unlike the pristine subways in Seoul or Tokyo, the subway system in New York is fairly loud and dirty, and it lacks basic facilities such as restrooms for passengers. The subway system in Seoul is excellent. It spans hundreds of miles of tracks in every corner of the Seoul metropolitan area and costs less than two dollars to ride. It even reaches the outer suburbs of Seoul. Subway cars in Seoul come often, and they are safe and clean. Each station has  restrooms and convenience stores, and the larger stations even have shops and boutiques. The subway in Tokyo is similar to the subway in Seoul. It's convenient, expansive, and inexpensive. It's important to be polite when riding the subway in Japan. Japanese people don't talk on the phone or eat food while riding the train. That is one difference between South Korea and Japan.

*pristine: in perfect condition; like new

**Following the Reading** Answer the questions.

1 What are the differences between American parents and Asian parents?

2 What are the similarities between Asian parents and parents in the Middle East?

3 What are the negative aspects of the New York City subway system?

4 What are the positive aspects of the Seoul and Tokyo subway systems?

**Paraphrasing a Preview and Summary of the Main Points** It's important to preview the main points of the speech at the end of the introduction. You should also summarize the main points at the beginning of the conclusion. Paraphrase the summary by using different words or expressions than you did in the preview.

A  Paraphrase the preview of the main points by using the given strategies in order to create a summary of the main points. Be sure to use the past simple tense.

> **Strategy 1** Use synonyms—different words with the same meanings—to replace words in the original passage.
>
> **Strategy 2** Change the order of some words or expressions in the sentence.

ex. To begin with, I will talk about the average American home.

→ *I mentioned the average American home at the beginning of my speech.*

1  Lastly, I want to talk about the roles of pets in households in Southeast Asia.

→

2  Next, I'd like to discuss a typical family dinner in Brazil.

→

3  After that, I'd like to tell you about some Mexican dishes that are very easy to prepare.

→

4  Finally, I would like to share three interesting places you can visit in London for free.

→

5  I will comment on European people's attitudes toward climate change after that.

→

6  Next, I will tell you about some hostels in Thailand that cost less than ten U.S. dollars per night.

→

7  I will share with you why Northern Europeans are so much happier than the rest of the world at the end of my talk.

→

8  Finally, I will discuss the working conditions of the average Russian twentysomething.

→

*talk about = mention, discuss, share, share with you, tell you about, comment on

B  Read the three main points in the body of Adam's speech. Then paraphrase a preview of the main points and a summary of the main points.

| End of the Introduction |
| --- |

Preview of Main Points (Use a future form: *will* or *be going to*.)

*To begin with, I will talk about...*

_____

| Body |
| --- |

First, let's talk about Thanksgiving in the United States. Thanksgiving is celebrated on the fourth Thursday in November each year. Traditionally, Thanksgiving was a day for Americans to give thanks for a plentiful harvest. In modern times, it is a day for Americans to give thanks for the blessings in their lives. The holiday is usually celebrated with family members or friends. Turkey with mashed potatoes and gravy are the most common dishes associated with Thanksgiving. Of course, a slice of pumpkin pie is the perfect ending to a great meal!

Now that I have discussed Thanksgiving in America, let's talk about Thanksgiving in Korea. Chuseok, Korean Thanksgiving, does not fall on the same day each year. It follows the lunar calendar. Similar to most harvest festivals, it is celebrated in the fall. In Korea, family members meet at the parent's home. Plenty of food and drinks are prepared for visitors. A common dessert served during Chuseok holiday is *songpyeon*. *Songpyeon* is a sweet rice cake containing honey or sugar in the center. Besides celebrating the harvest, Chuseok is a time to pay respect to the family's ancestors. One method of paying respect involves visiting the gravesites of deceased relatives and making sure the areas look beautiful and well-manicured.

I've talked about Korea's Thanksgiving festival. So now I'd like to discuss Thanksgiving in Canada. In Canada, Thanksgiving is celebrated much the same way it is in the United States. Canada's Thanksgiving, however, is not celebrated on the fourth Thursday in November. Canadian Thanksgiving is celebrated on the second Monday in October. Canadians get together with family members and enjoy a large feast. They eat and give thanks for the plentiful harvest and other blessings that they have experienced over the past year. A Thanksgiving feast in Canada might look similar to one in the United States. Turkey, mashed potatoes, and pumpkin pie will probably be on the menu. I have discussed Thanksgiving in Canada. Now, I'd like to summarize my talk.

| Beginning of the Conclusion |
| --- |

Summary of Main Points (Use the past simple tense.)

*First, I mentioned...*

_____

#### 🎯 Common Mistakes  Talking about a Country's Food

| | |
| --- | --- |
| Mexico food (incorrect) | Mexican food (correct) |
| Japan food (incorrect) | Japanese food (correct) |

# Do It Yourself

## The Informative Speech: How Different Countries or Cultures Perceive a Specific Topic

Now it is time for you to do it yourself! Use the information you learned in the previous sections in order to create an outline for a speech explaining how different countries or cultures perceive a topic.

A Create an outline for the speech in the spaces below. Talk about one topic and how it is viewed in three different locations in the world.

| Attention-Getting Opener |
|---|

Which strategy would you choose for your attention-getting opener?

☐ shocking statistic ☐ rhetorical question ☐ anecdote

☐ famous quote ☐ visual aid ☐ gimmick

Now, write your attention-getting opener.

_____

_____

Preview of Main Points:

Transition 1:

Main Point 1 (Location 1):

Transition 2:

Main Point 2 (Location 2):

Transition 3:

Main Point 3 (Location 3):

Transition 4:

Summary of Main Points:

Concluding Remarks:

_____

B Give a short speech about how different countries or cultures view a specific topic. Use your notes from A.

# Checklist

1 What is the benefit of providing a contrast between different locations in a speech?

2 Although it is not a rule, how many main points are usually used in a speech?

3 What comes at the end of the introduction? How about the beginning of the conclusion?

4 What two strategies regarding paraphrasing are mentioned in the unit?

## Presentation Tips

### Practice Makes Perfect

Public speaking can be very challenging, especially when anxiety or nervousness becomes an issue. One of the most common symptoms associated with nervousness during a speech is going blank. Going blank means completely forgetting everything that was prepared beforehand. The harder the speaker tries to remember the words, the farther away they seem to float. It can be so traumatic that some speakers will quit right in the middle of their speeches. Others, in an attempt to avoid this situation, go to extreme measures and read or memorize their speeches. But reading or memorizing a speech is not a desired method of delivery. A speech should be well prepared, but it should also feel natural and conversational. In order to achieve this desired result, speakers should use a method of delivery known as the extemporaneous delivery. In order to deliver a great extemporaneous speech, speakers need to rehearse. A person should spend at least a week going over the speech in front of a mirror or with a close friend or roommate. One can even record the speech with a smartphone and then watch it. Rehearsing the speech well is the best antidote to getting nervous and going blank.

# Past, Present, and Future

## Warm-up

Look at the evolution of these common objects and make predictions about what they will be like in the future.

| Past | Present | Future |
| --- | --- | --- |
| | | **?** |
| | | **?** |
| | | **?** |
| | | **?** |

**In the Past, Now, and in the Future** When giving a past, present, and future speech, you should provide examples of how things were in the past, how they are now, and how you imagine they might be in the future. This will give audience members a better understanding of the topic.

## Vocabulary

A  Read the sentences and choose the best answers.

1  The first automobile was invented in the late 1800s; however, automobiles weren't mass-produced until the early ($19^{th}$ century / $20^{th}$ century).

2  Our school hasn't remodeled the buildings in (ages / months). They look exactly the same as they did when my brother graduated three years ago.

3  The (first / latest) generation smartphone had less memory and a much slower processor than current ones.

4  In the 1950s, children were active and spent a lot of time playing outside. In the (golden / modern) age, children are much more likely to stay inside and to play video games or watch television.

5  Carmakers are now designing new cars that look like (old-fashioned / futuristic) cars from the 1950s and '60s.

6  Technology is advancing at such a fast pace these days that (contemporary / ancient) technology is usually out of date within six months of its release.

B  **Pair work** | Ask and answer the questions with a partner.

| | |
|---|---|
| | classic cars or modern cars? |
| | classical music or contemporary music? |
| Do you prefer... | classic literature or modern literature? |
| | classic films or modern films? |
| | (Your Items) |

A I think classic cars are much cooler than modern cars.
B Yes, I agree. Classic cars have more beautiful designs than modern cars.

## Grammar

A  Let's learn to talk about the future by using *will* and *be going to*.

| will (prediction) | be going to (plan) |
|---|---|
| I believe everyone **will** be using some form of public transportation by 2030. | The city **is going to** begin construction on the new community center in 2020. |
| I think all gaming in the future **will** take place in the virtual reality world. | The company **is going to** release its new smartwatch in November of next year. |

B  Create your own sentences by using *will* and *be going to*.

1

2

3

**Compare and Contrast the Past, Present, and Future** There are important expressions that you can use to compare and contrast the past, present, and future. It is useful to compare and contrast the past, present, and future because it shows how things have changed and how they might change in the future.

## Language Patterns

A  Let's learn some expressions.

1  For the past, present, and future...

| Past | Present | Future |
|------|---------|--------|
| in the past | right now | in the near future |
| long ago / ages ago | currently | in the distant future |
| back then / back in the day | in modern times | in the years to come |
| at an earlier time | in contemporary times | (number) years from now |

2  For comparing and contrasting...

| Compare | | Contrast | |
|---------|--|----------|--|
| also | again | on the contrary, | on the other hand, |
| as well | too | yet, | however, |

B  Compare and contrast the topics below from a past to present perspective and a present to future perspective.

• automobiles    • homes    • education    • computers    • work    • dating /marriage

*Ages ago, people traveled by horse and buggy. Currently, however, people travel by car. In the near future, I think people will also travel by car. In the distant future, on the other hand, I think people will probably use self-driving cars.*

## Pronunciation 🔊

A  Read and listen to the sentences below. Then practice the common reduction of the /t/ and /j/ sounds.

| ending sound /t/ + beginning sound /j/ = /tʃ/ sound |
|---|

Don't you think Fred's new sports car is cool?

Car companies want you to feel loyalty toward their car brands.

I couldn't have overcome my fear of public speaking without your help.

B  Listen and practice. Be careful when pronouncing the ending sound /t/ with the beginning sound /j/.

A  Don't you think the campus looks exactly like it did when we were students?

B  It looks just like it did ten years ago.

A  Look down there! That's where you put your handprints in the wet cement sidewalk.

B  I remember. Where are your handprints?

A  Don't you remember? I was too scared to do it.

**Interesting Details about the Past and Present** When writing a past, present, and future speech, you should give the audience interesting details about your topic in the past and now. A well-researched speech will contain interesting details that pique the interest of the audience and draw them in to your talk.

## Reading 🔊

Read about how baseball has changed.

Baseball is sometimes referred to as America's pastime because it was invented in the USA. Professional baseball players in the early 20th century did not earn much money, so they often took part-time jobs as farmhands and construction workers in order to earn extra money during the off-season. In the early days of baseball, teams played fewer games in a season than they do now. The balls were also softer, so games were less exciting. Babe Ruth is the most famous baseball player from this era. In 1927, he hit 60 home runs in one season, a record which wasn't broken for 34 years. In 1961, Roger Maris, an outfielder for the New York Yankees, hit 61 home runs, breaking Ruth's record for the most home runs in a single season. In the golden age of baseball, which took place from the 1920s to the 1960s, players began to earn more money and gained more recognition. At this time, the league switched to a harder ball, which allowed players to hit the ball harder and further. This added excitement to the games because there were more home runs. Great players such as Joe DiMaggio, Mickey Mantle, and Hank Aaron became superstars in the sport during this era. Fans were even interested in players' private lives. When Joe DiMaggio, perhaps the most famous major-leaguer from this era, married movie star Marilyn Monroe in 1954, it was headline news. The marriage, however, did not last long. They divorced only 274 days later. In the modern age, baseball is still hugely popular; however, it must compete with other sports such as American football and basketball. In the years to come, I imagine Americans will still love baseball. Children will still play in their yards or at the nearest park, and fans of Major League Baseball will still attend games and cheer for their home teams. And, of course, players will continue to make millions of dollars playing America's pastime.

**Following the Reading** Change the incorrect statements into correct statements.

1 Baseball games became less exciting when the league switched to harder baseballs.

2 Babe Ruth hit 60 home runs in 1927. His record was broken by Joe DiMaggio in 1961.

3 The golden age of baseball was from the 1970s to the 1980s.

4 Players earned more money and recognition in the early 20th century.

5 Hank Aaron married Marilyn Monroe in 1954, but the wedding did not last long.

**Concluding Remarks** Every speech needs a strong conclusion. The conclusion consists of two parts: a summary of the main points and concluding remarks. Strong concluding remarks will leave a lasting positive impression on an audience. There are several strategies you can use to write a strong conclusion.

A   Match the concluding remarks strategies to the correct examples.

> a  Make a prediction.
>
> b  Make a reference to your opening.
>
> c  Make a call to action.
>
> d  Answer a question that you asked in your opening.
>
> e  Complete a story or an anecdote that you started in the introduction.

(1) As I mentioned in the beginning of my speech, Enzo Ferrari said, "The fact is I don't drive just to get from A to B. I enjoy feeling the car's reaction, becoming part of it." As self-driving technology becomes the new standard, many of us will miss the ability to operate the magnificent machines great carmakers have built.

(2) I'd like to finish my story about that shy little boy who had trouble making eye contact. Well, that little boy was me. It took years for me to build my confidence and to overcome my fear of public speaking. But here I am today, proudly speaking to all of you.

(3) I began my speech by asking you how many hours per year you think the average American spends in traffic. Well, the answer to that question is 42 hours. Think about a future without traffic jams. Just imagine what better things we could be doing with that time.

(4) In the future, we need to fight for equality regardless of a person's race, gender, or sexual orientation. Visit the website www.socialjusticeforall.org to find your local chapter. Take the time to get involved. Help build a better future for our children.

(5) I believe virtual reality is the future of gaming. I imagine a future where gamers are connected in a virtual reality world with an endless number of gaming options. I see a place where gamers from all corners of the globe can connect with one another in a magical gaming paradise.

B  Read the introduction and the body of a speech about dating services in the past, present, and future. Then write concluding remarks by using one of the strategies in A.

Dating apps have made finding a partner easier than ever before. In fact, I used a dating app recently to help me meet someone who also lives in my area of the city. We met at a local café and had a great conversation. Today, I'm going to talk about dating services in the past, dating services today, and what I think dating services will be like in the future.

First, let's talk about dating services in the past. In the 1980s, few people had Internet connections. In order to use a dating service, you had to visit the office of one of several dating services, create a profile, and make a tape. Your dating profile included information about you as well as the qualities you were looking for in a partner. Your tape let members see what you looked like, and gave them a glimpse into your personality. Once your profile and tape were made, the company tried to find matches by using the information in members' profiles and on their videotapes. This method was very labor intensive, time consuming, and expensive. But some good matches were made, and many members are still happily married to this day.

Now that I have discussed dating services in the past, let me move on to the topic of dating services today. Dating services like the ones I have just described started disappearing in the late 1990s and early 2000s. They were replaced by dating apps. Dating apps let you create dating profiles that can become part of dating app databases. Users download the apps and view the profiles on the databases. Search engines allow users to screen out bad matches. If users find profiles that match their preferences, they send text messages to the people they would like to see. Some apps require paid membership, however, others are free.

Now that I have finished discussing dating services in the present, let's briefly discuss what dating services might look like in the future. I'm not exactly sure what dating services will be like in the future. I think virtual reality dating will open up a whole new kind of dating because users will be able to invent avatars with entirely different appearances and personalities. This might also bring with it a lot of problems. How will we be able to trust the people we meet in the virtual reality world?

Now that I have shared my opinions about dating services in the future, I would like to summarize my talk. First, I talked about dating services in the past. Then, I discussed dating services in the present. Finally, I talked about dating services in the future. (Concluding Remarks)

🖐 **Common Mistakes  century vs. Century**

a century (correct)          the 20<sup>th</sup> century (correct)          the 20<sup>th</sup> Century (incorrect)

## Do It Yourself

**The Informative Speech: The Past, Present, and Future**   Now it is time for you to do it yourself! Use the information you learned in the previous sections in order to create an outline for a speech explaining the past, present, and future as it relates to a topic of your choice.

A   Create an outline for the speech in the spaces below. Use a past, present, and future organizational pattern to talk about your choice of topic.

| Attention-Getting Opener |
| --- |

Which strategy would you choose for your attention-getting opener?
- ☐ shocking statistic
- ☐ famous quote
- ☐ rhetorical question
- ☐ visual aid
- ☐ anecdote
- ☐ gimmick

Now, write your attention-getting opener.

_____

_____

Preview of Main Points:

Transition 1:

Main Point 1 (Past):

Transition 2:

Main Point 2 (Present):

Transition 3:

Main Point 3 (Future):

Transition 4:

Summary of Main Points:

| Concluding Remarks |
| --- |

Which strategy would you choose for your concluding remarks?
- ☐ prediction
- ☐ reference your opening
- ☐ call to action
- ☐ answer a question
- ☐ complete a story

Now, write your concluding remarks.

_____

B   Give a short speech on any topic by using a past, present, and future organizational pattern. Use your notes from A.

# Checklist

1 In a past, present, future speech, what is the benefit of providing the audience with examples from different time periods?

2 Why is it useful to compare and contrast the past, present, and future?

3 What are the benefits of including interesting and well-researched details in a speech?

4 What are the two parts of the conclusion?

5 How does writing a strong conclusion improve a speech?

6 Name the strategies mentioned in the unit for writing strong concluding remarks.

---

**Presentation Tips**

### Bookending the Opening and Closing

Three of the concluding remarks strategies discussed in this unit are what you call bookends. When you bookend the opening and the closing, it means you have purposely connected them. Bookending is an excellent way to bring your talk full circle. It also has the added benefit of making the audience feel smart because you are asking them to remember something that was mentioned at the beginning of the speech and is relevant now during the closing. The three strategies discussed in this unit are:

• complete a story that you began telling in the opening
• make a reference to your opening comments
• answer a question that you asked in your opening

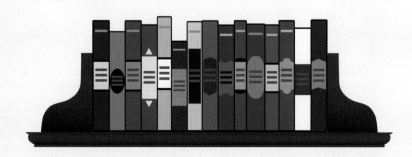

# Problems and Solutions

## Warm-up

A  Match the societal problems with the correct pictures. You can choose the terms that you think work best.

a    Pollution        b    Addiction        c    Poverty

B    Which societal problem above do you believe is the most serious?

**Identifying Problems** In a speech with a problem and solutions organizational pattern, you must first decide what kind of problem you would like to address. There are plenty of societal problems to choose from, but don't forget about local issues. These include problems at school or in the workplace.

## Vocabulary

A  Complete the sentences with the correct words from the word box.

| unemployment | income inequality | racism | bullying | obesity | sexism |
|---|---|---|---|---|---|

1 _____ persists in the United States despite the work of civil rights activists such as Dr. Martin Luther King and Rosa Parks.

2 _____ is a problem that has increased in the past forty years. The result is an enormous amount of wealth in a small number of hands.

3 _____ in the workplace is a problem in many offices. Women across the globe are fed up with being harassed by male coworkers or bosses.

4 Online _____ is a big problem in the technological age. One out of three children aged 10 or older report being harassed online by classmates or peers.

5 Youth _____ is a societal problem that affects recent college graduates who want to find good jobs and start families.

6 The consumption of too many sweetened drinks is thought to be a big contributing factor to the _____ epidemic.

B  **Pair work** | Choose one of the issues below and ask your partner how concerned he or she is about that problem.

- Bullying
- Unemployment
- Income inequality
- Obesity epidemic
- Racism
- Sexism

A How concerned are you about school bullying?

B I'm very concerned about school bullying. I think it's a big problem in a lot of schools...

## Grammar

A  Let's learn about the defining relative pronouns *who*, *which*, *where*, and *that*.

| who (person) | which (thing) | where (place) | that |
|---|---|---|---|
| Dr. Lee is a doctor **who** helps people with emotional problems. | We proposed solutions **which** might change the world. | We visited the city **where** flooding had destroyed the houses. | (***That*** can be used instead of *who* or *which*.) |

B  Complete the sentences by using *who*, *which*, *where*, or *that*.

1 Bangladesh is a country _____ rising sea levels could cause millions of homes to flood.

2 Sienna's father is the kind of person _____ must help people when they are in need.

3 Poverty is a problem _____ affects one billion people in the world.

4 Addiction is a societal problem _____ doesn't have a simple solution.

**Definitions** When giving a problem and solutions speech, it is important to operationally define the problem. We do this because audience members might not be familiar with your topic. Write your definition based on the ideas and opinions of the experts in the field.

## Language Patterns

A  Let's learn about operationally defining terms in a speech.

| Operational Definitions |
| --- |
| Poverty **can be defined as** earning less than $12,500 per year. |
| The term alcoholism **refers to** an addiction to alcohol and an inability to function without it. |
| Racism **is defined as** discriminatory actions or policies that are based on a person's skin color. |

B  Write operational definitions for the terms in the table by using the expressions in A. You may use your dictionary in order to find definitions for the terms.

| Term | Definition |
| --- | --- |
| Bullying | *Bullying can be defined as the constant harassment or torment of a child by his or her peers for an extended period of time.* |
| Unemployment | |
| Obesity | |
| Drought | |
| Discrimination | |

## Pronunciation 🔊

A  Read and listen to the words below. Then practice the pronunciations of the /v/ and /w/ sounds.

| /v/ | /w/ |
| --- | --- |
| various | weather |
| poverty | while |
| vicious | winter |
| living | with |
| universal | wage |

B  Listen and practice. Be careful when pronouncing the /v/ and /w/ sounds.

1  **We** li**v**e on a planet **w**here millions of people are stuck in a cycle of **v**icious po**v**erty.

2  Climate change means li**v**ing **w**ith longer **w**inters and more extreme summers.

3  **V**arious societal problems need to be addressed **w**hile **w**e still ha**v**e time to solve them.

**Solutions as Main Points** When writing a problem and solutions speech, you should operationally define the problem in the introduction. Then, let your solutions to the problem become the main points in the body of your speech. This will give the audience a clear outline of your various solutions.

## Reading 🔊

Read about the societal problem and some possible solutions.

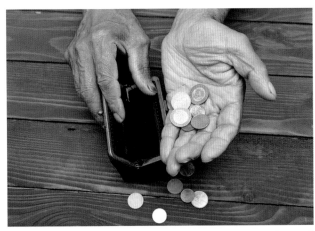

Roughly 40% of Americans live in poverty. Living in poverty can be defined as being under the age of 65 and earning less than $12,500 per year. Experts have attempted to come up with solutions to the problem of poverty in the United States. Today, I'd like to discuss two of these solutions with you. The first is the universal basic income (UBI). The second solution is raising the minimum wage to $15 per hour. First, let me talk about the universal basic income. When someone is in poverty, that person struggles to find enough money to pay rent and buy food. With UBI, the government would give a certain amount of money to everyone to cover basic expenses. People would have to work for extra perks such as nicer clothes, a nicer house, or better food. Their basic needs, however, would always be taken care of in this system. Some people argue that if you give people money, they'll stop working. It's hard to say if this is true because UBI has never been tried on a large scale. I guess we'll have to wait and see. Now that I have discussed UBI, I'd like to talk about a $15 minimum wage. The average worker works 40 hours per week. At $15 per hour, a worker working 40 hours per week would earn approximately $30,000 per year. This would be well above the poverty threshold in the United States. Some people argue that a $15 minimum wage would hurt small business owners who wouldn't be able to afford employees at this rate. Although some small businesses would be hurt, a majority of low-wage workers work in the service sector for large, profitable corporations. These companies can afford to pay their workers $15 per hour. These two solutions are currently being discussed in the United States. It will be interesting to see which one of these solutions gains traction with the public and perhaps someday becomes law.

*perks: extra benefits
*threshold: the edge of; the verge of
*gain traction: to make progress; to move forward confidently

**Following the Reading** Answer the questions.

1 According to the reading, what is the definition of poverty?

2 What two solutions to the poverty problem are suggested in the article?

3 How much would a person making $15 per hour and working 40 hours per week earn in a year?

4 What argument do critics of a $15 per hour minimum wage make?

**Using PowerPoint Slides: Four Important Pieces of Advice** Visual aids can enhance the quality of any speech or presentation. But it is also very easy to misuse this technology. Below are four pieces of advice you should follow when using PowerPoint slides in a speech.

**A** Read the four pieces of advice regarding PowerPoint slides. Then put a check in the box that matches the piece of advice.

1 Use key words and phrases with easy-to-read fonts which can be read from the back of the room.

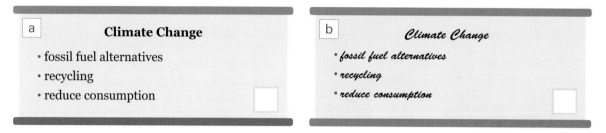

2 Use a unified color scheme that coordinates well with the other slides. Using the same color slides is okay.

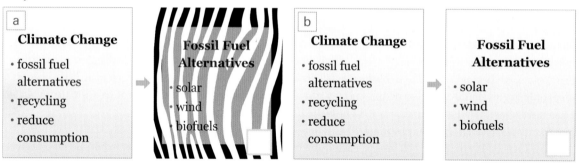

3 Use bullet points, lettering, or numbering in the slides in order to help you organize your points of discussion.

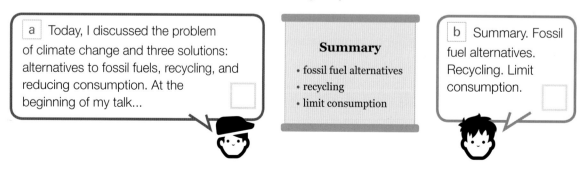

4 Use your slides as a guide to delivering the message in your own words.

B Fill in the blanks in the presentation slides with correct information from the speech.

A close friend of mine struggled with alcohol addiction for years. In college, she drank socially at parties and bars. As time went by, her drinking became a serious problem. Today, I'd like to talk about addiction and some possible solutions. First, I'll talk about 12-step programs. Next, I will discuss therapy. Last, I will tell you about the importance of maintaining personal connections.

To begin, let me talk about 12-step programs. 12-step programs seem to work for two reasons. First, they are effective because they keep the members of the group accountable. Group members share their daily successes and failures with the group. The feedback and support they receive motivate them. The second reason is that sponsors provide valuable assistance. A sponsor is someone the alcoholic can call anytime, day or night. The sponsor will then help him or her by offering advice, support, or a sympathetic ear.

Now that I have discussed 12-step programs, I'd like to discuss therapy as a treatment for addiction. Addiction can often be the result of a traumatic incident in the past. It is possible that the person suffering from addiction may not even be aware of this past trauma. A qualified therapist can help a patient suffering from addiction deal with his or her past trauma. When the patient is able to address or even resolve a serious issue from the past, his or her addiction becomes more treatable.

Now that I have discussed therapy, I'd like to mention the idea of maintaining meaningful personal connections. Johann Hari, author of *Chasing the Scream: The First and the Last Days of the War on Drugs*, states that addiction is often the result of a lack of connection to anything meaningful in the addict's life. Maintaining meaningful connections to family and friends is an essential part of our humanity. If we lose that, we may find ourselves more likely to become addicted to substances such as alcohol.

Now that I've discussed the importance of staying connected, I'd like to summarize my speech. First, I discussed 12-step programs. Then, I talked about individual and group therapy. Finally, I mentioned the importance of staying connected. In the beginning of my talk, I told you about my friend, who has struggled with alcohol addiction since university. I'm happy to tell you that due to a combination of all three solutions mentioned in this speech today, she has been able to overcome her alcohol addiction. She hasn't had a drink in more than three years.

---

**Treating** [1]_____

- 12 Step Programs
- therapy
- maintaining personal connections

---

**12 Step Programs**

- keep members
  [2]_____
- sponsors provide valuable
  [3]_____

---

**Therapy**

- result of [4]_____ trauma
- addiction more
  [5]_____ if past trauma resolved

---

**Staying Connected**

- addiction related to a lack of [6]_____ connections
- addiction more [7]_____ without strong connections

---

[8]_____

- 12 Step Programs
- therapy
- maintaining connections

## Do It Yourself

**The Informative Speech: Problems and Solutions**  Now it is time for you to do it yourself! Use the information you learned in the previous sections in order to create an outline for a speech explaining a problem and offering solutions.

A  Create an outline for the speech in the spaces below. Identify a problem you would like to discuss. Then use a problem and solutions organizational pattern to talk about your topic.

| Attention-Getting Opener |
| --- |

Which strategy would you choose for your attention-getting opener?

☐ shocking statistic          ☐ rhetorical question          ☐ anecdote
☐ famous quote               ☐ visual aid                    ☐ gimmick

Now, write your attention-getting opener.

_____

_____

Preview of Main Points:

Transition 1:

Main Point 1 (Solution 1):

Transition 2:

Main Point 2 (Solution 2):

Transition 3:

Main Point 3 (Solution 3):

Transition 4:

Summary of Main Points:

| Concluding Remarks |
| --- |

Which strategy would you choose for your concluding remarks?

☐ prediction               ☐ call to action           ☐ complete a story
☐ reference your opening   ☐ answer a question

Now, write your concluding remarks.

_____

B  Give a short speech on any topic by using a problem and solutions organizational pattern. Use your notes from A.

# Checklist

1  When choosing a topic for a problem and solutions speech, what kinds of topics should you not forget to consider?

2  Why should you operationally define a problem in a problem and solutions speech?

3  When writing a problem and solutions speech, how should you organize the body?

4  What four pieces of advice are mentioned in the unit with regard to using PowerPoint slides?

**Presentation Tips**

### Dos and Don'ts Regarding the Use of Slides

There are a few more dos and don'ts you should consider when using slides in a speech. First, do make sure that every word is spelled correctly. It is unacceptable in this day and age to have a spelling mistake on a slide in a speech. Not only does it diminish your credibility as a speaker, but it also makes you look lazy. If you cannot be bothered to spend ten extra seconds to look up a word on the Internet, then what other shortcuts have you taken in preparation for your speech?

Second, don't use video or audio unless it is absolutely necessary for your speech. We are all familiar with Murphy's Law: If something can go wrong, it probably will. It is especially true when it comes to using an audio or video clip. There could be a formatting issue with a computer, a volume button could be muted, or a file could have been deleted. If you are going to use audio or video, arrive at the classroom or boardroom early in order to ensure that all of your files are working correctly. With a little due diligence, you can avoid a big embarrassment.

# Cause and Effect I

## Warm-up

Choose the arrows that lead from causes to effects.

**Emotions** When giving a cause-and-effects speech, it is a good idea to learn some vocabulary that describes emotions. We do this because we can link emotional states to specific causes. Once you have chosen a topic, ask yourself what emotional effects might result from it.

## Vocabulary

A Match the vocabulary from the word bank with the correct definitions.

| satisfaction | disappointment | desire | frustration |
| --- | --- | --- | --- |
| accomplishment | perseverance | devastation | depression |

1 _____ : a feeling of achievement or success

2 _____ : a strong feeling of want or need for something

3 _____ : a strong feeling of annoyance over the inability to change or accomplish something

4 _____ : great damage or destruction

5 _____ : the feeling of having one's expectations, wishes, or needs met

6 _____ : a feeling of great sadness and despair

7 _____ : not giving up or quitting something even though it is difficult to achieve

8 _____ : a feeling of sadness caused by the inability to achieve one's hopes or dreams

B **Pair work** | **Ask your partner to think of a possible cause for the following emotional states.**

| accomplishment | depression | disappointment | frustration |
| --- | --- | --- | --- |

A What do you think can cause a person to feel a sense of accomplishment?

B Graduating from university might give you a feeling of accomplishment.

## Grammar

A Let's learn about the suffixes *-ment*, *-ion*, and *-ance*.

| Verbs | | Nouns (with suffix) | |
| --- | --- | --- | --- |
| accomplish | disappoint | accomplish**ment** | disappoint**ment** |
| depress | frustrate | depress**ion** | frustrat**ion** |
| satisfy | persevere | satisfact**ion** | persever**ance** |

B **Read the sentences. Then write the correct verb or noun forms of the words in the blanks.**

1 When Julia was rejected from her first choice of university, a wave of _____ washed over her. (disappoint)

2 Parents shouldn't do everything for their children. Kids need to feel the _____ that occurs when they _____ something difficult. (satisfy / accomplish)

3 One's ability to _____, even when things are very difficult, is an honorable quality in a person. (persevere)

4 Do you believe that constant _____ can eventually lead to _____? (frustrate / depress)

**A Cause and Its Effects**  When giving a cause-and-effects speech, it is helpful to learn some expressions for describing a cause and its effects. We use these expressions in order to clearly communicate to the audience what the exact cause is and what some of the effects of that cause are.

## Language Patterns

A  Read and practice the different expressions for describing a cause and its effects.

| Cause > Effect | |
| --- | --- |
| give rise to    bring about    result in<br>cause    create    lead to    produce | As a result    Consequently    Due to this<br>Because of this    On account of this    Since doing this |
| Learning a foreign language **gives rise to** improved cognitive skills, more job opportunities, and strong feelings of accomplishment. | I studied Spanish for seven years. **As a result**, I saw an improvement in my cognitive skills, received more job opportunities, and experienced a strong feeling of accomplishment. |

B  Write activities in the left column and three effects of it in the right column. Then describe the cause-and-effect relationship between the two columns by using the expressions in A.

| Activity | 3 Effects |
| --- | --- |
| *Playing Sports* | *better teamwork skills, increased confidence, and higher fitness levels* |
|  |  |
|  |  |
|  |  |

ex. 1  *Playing sports produces better teamwork skills, increased confidence, and higher fitness levels in people.*

ex. 2  *I play soccer. Consequently, I have better teamwork skills, increased confidence, and higher fitness levels than I would have if I didn't play.*

## Pronunciation 🔊

A  Read and listen to the words below. Then practice the pronunciations of these three diphthongs.

| /aɪ/ | /eɪ/ | /aʊ/ |
| --- | --- | --- |
| **I** | play | now |
| rise | great | how |
| write | stay | account |
| my | make | sound |

B  Listen and practice. Be careful when pronouncing these diphthongs.

1  In m**y** opinion, investing a little money n**ow** will give r**i**se to a gr**ea**ter fortune in the future.

2  If you want to improve your overall fitness level, d**ow**nload a fitness-tracking appli**ca**tion to your smartphone and m**a**ke l**i**festyle changes ba**se**d on its recommend**a**tions.

3  **I** want to learn h**ow** to speak French, but **I** don't think **I** have enough t**i**me to t**a**ke a class.

**The Benefits**  The most important aspect of the speech is the body. When giving a cause-and-effects speech, you need to provide good supporting details for the main points in the body of your speech. Good supporting details demonstrate that you are a well-informed speaker and a credible source of the information you are sharing.

# Reading 🔊

A  Read the article about the benefits of regular exercise.

According to a 2008 German study about exercise and aging, the average person can expect to live 4.3 to 8 years longer by exercising regularly. Although there are a multitude of benefits associated with regular exercise, I'd like to share two interesting ones with you today. First, you can reduce stress through exercise. Second, exercising regularly might boost your immune system. First, let's talk about reducing stress. Exercise releases endorphins in your brain. Endorphins are chemicals that regulate your sleep and act as natural painkillers in your body. Exercise helps your body release more of these chemicals, which, in turn, help you sleep better and experience less physical pain throughout the day and night. The effect is that your overall stress levels decrease and you can better deal with life's unexpected daily challenges. Next, I'd like to discuss how exercising might be responsible for boosting your immune system. There are two convincing explanations on why exercise helps our bodies fight illness. The first theory is that exercise circulates white blood cells, or antibodies, throughout the body more rapidly. Because of this, white blood cells are able to detect infections more quickly. The second theory is that exercise slows down the production of stress hormones, the hormones most responsible for causing infections and illnesses. By reducing stress and inflammation, the body remains in a better state of overall health. I have told you about two of the positive effects associated with exercise. I hope this article has inspired you to find the time to get at least thirty minutes of exercise per day. This small change could have all kinds of positive effects on your overall health.

*inflammation: a physical reaction to an infection or injury which results in swelling, hotness, or pain

**Following the Reading**  Read the statements and mark them True or False.

1  Exercise can reduce stress and may even boost one's immune system.                [True / False]

2  Endorphins released during exercise prevent a person from sleeping.                [True / False]

3  Exercise causes antibodies to move more slowly throughout the body.                [True / False]

4  A person who exercises regularly may experience less inflammation because exercise slows down the production of stress hormones.                [True / False]

B  Do you exercise regularly? If so, what benefits do you experience from doing regular exercise?

**Using Charts and Graphs** When explaining data to an audience, the use of too many numbers can make the explanation confusing for listeners. By creating a visual representation to go along with the data, you are providing the audience with visual cues which will help them understand the information more clearly.

A  Match the chart and graph descriptions to the correct examples. Write the letters in the boxes.

a  We use this kind of chart to show proportions. If you want to visually express what percentages of a whole certain entities control, you should use this kind of chart.

b  This kind of chart is the most visually appealing to an audience. Each individual picture represents a value, so the more times the picture is repeated on the chart, the larger the volume of that particular value is.

c  This kind of chart is great for showing relationships between two or more groups. In this kind of chart, each group is represented by a column with the height of the column indicating the range.

d  Although this kind of chart is not the most visually appealing, it is excellent for showing a range of high or low points in a certain time period.

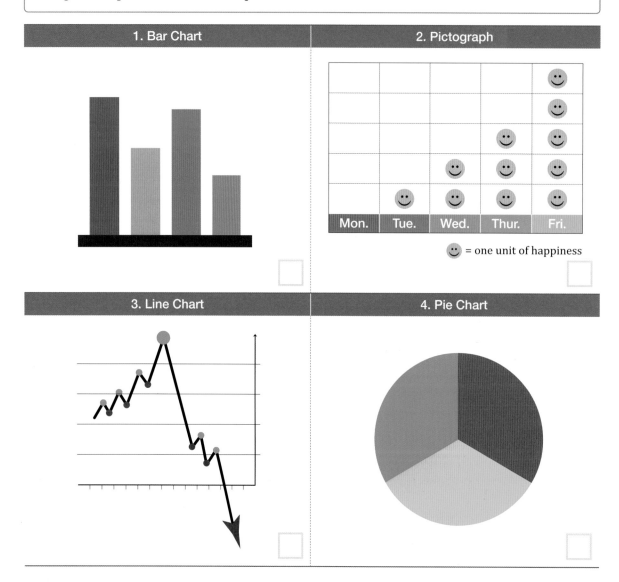

| 1. Bar Chart | 2. Pictograph |

= one unit of happiness

| 3. Line Chart | 4. Pie Chart |

B  Create visuals by using the speeches in the left column. Use the examples in A to create your charts and graphs below.

| | | |
|---|---|---|
| 1 | I'd like to talk about how high school students' interest in sports has changed over the past twenty years in the United States and Canada. In 1998, 49% of students expressed interest in playing team sports. In 2008, that number had dropped to 33%. By 2018, only 25% of students expressed interest in playing team sports. | **Bar Chart** |
| 2 | Let's talk about foreign language enrollment at Icarus University in Arizona, USA. 31% of the students enrolled in a foreign language class study Spanish. 24% study German. Just below German is Chinese at 23%. 15% study French, and 4% study Korean. 3% study various other languages. | **Pie Chart** |
| 3 | As you can see, popularity in the social networking application Zinger increased dramatically in 2017 to 400,000 users worldwide. But in 2018, interest in the app decreased dramatically to about 200,000 users. In 2019, use of the app stabilized at about 210,000 users worldwide. | **Line Chart** |
| 4 | Here are the preferred exercise times for the employees working at the XYZ Company who exercise regularly. 40 of these men and women prefer working out in the morning. Half, 20 employees, like exercising at lunchtime. Most of them, 60 people, enjoy exercising in the evening. None of them likes to exercise at night. | **Pictograph** |

| Morning | Afternoon | Evening | Night |
|---|---|---|---|

= 20 employees

# Do It Yourself

**The Informative Speech: A Cause and Its Effects** Now it is time for you to do it yourself! Use the information you learned in the previous sections in order to create an outline for a speech explaining a cause and its effects.

A Create an outline for the speech in the spaces below. Choose any cause and its effects (including only two main points is okay). Then use a cause-and-effects organizational pattern to talk about your topic.

| Attention-Getting Opener |
|---|

Which strategy would you choose for your attention-getting opener?
- ☐ shocking statistic
- ☐ famous quote
- ☐ rhetorical question
- ☐ visual aid
- ☐ anecdote
- ☐ gimmick

Now, write an attention-getting opener which reveals your topic (a cause) in an interesting way.

_____

_____

Preview of Main Points:

Transition 1:

Main Point 1 (Effect 1):

Transition 2:

Main Point 2 (Effect 2):

Transition 3:

Main Point 3 (Effect 3):

Transition 4:

Summary of Main Points:

| Concluding Remarks |
|---|

Which strategy would you choose for your concluding remarks?
- ☐ prediction
- ☐ reference your opening
- ☐ call to action
- ☐ answer a question
- ☐ complete a story

Now, write your concluding remarks.

_____

B Give a short speech in which you describe a cause and its effects. Use your notes from A. Try to include a chart or graph in your speech in order to explain any relevant supporting data.

# Checklist

1 Why should we learn vocabulary that describes emotions in a cause-and-effects speech?
2 Why is it helpful to learn expressions for describing a cause and its effects?
3 Why do you need to provide good supporting details in the body of a speech?
4 What kinds of cues are you providing the audience with when you include a chart or graph?

## Presentation Tips

### Be Yourself!

I am sure we have all witnessed a classmate or coworker give an amazing speech filled with humor and wonderful anecdotes that had the entire crowd roaring with laughter. Although adding humor to a speech is fine, oftentimes, an entertainingly funny speech is a function of the personality of the speaker, not the language in the speech. The fact is that some people are just born funny. It is pointless to try to imitate a funny speaker in the hope that some of it will rub off on you. The better approach is to be the best "you" you can be. If you are a serious person, be serious. If you are sarcastic, find a way to include your sarcastic sensibilities in the speech. Audiences have an uncanny ability to detect a fraud. Instead of trying to be a hilarious public speaker like your coworker Carl or your classmate Amanda, be the down-to-earth, serious deep thinker that you are. As long as you are well prepared and authentic, the audience will respond positively to your speech.

# Cause and Effect II

## Warm-up

A  Read the comments and check the best match for each of them.

*I did an internship at my local hospital because...*

**1**

| a | my father, who is a doctor, inspired me a lot. | |
| b | my father, who is a salesman, inspired me a lot. | |
| c | my father, who is an engineer, inspired me a lot. | |

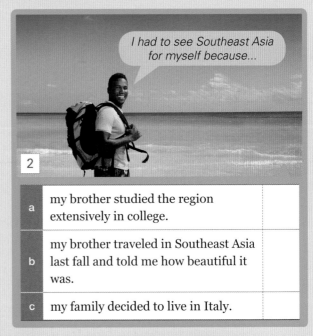

*I had to see Southeast Asia for myself because...*

**2**

| a | my brother studied the region extensively in college. | |
| b | my brother traveled in Southeast Asia last fall and told me how beautiful it was. | |
| c | my family decided to live in Italy. | |

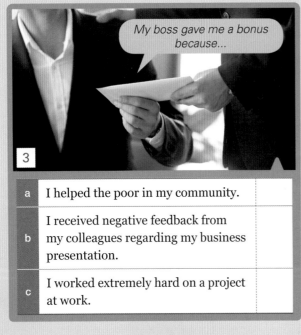

*My boss gave me a bonus because...*

**3**

| a | I helped the poor in my community. | |
| b | I received negative feedback from my colleagues regarding my business presentation. | |
| c | I worked extremely hard on a project at work. | |

*I decided to get a bachelor's degree in environmental science because...*

**4**

| a | I've always been interested in ancient civilizations. | |
| b | I want to work for a major tech company. | |
| c | I want to help solve the climate change crisis. | |

B  Who in your life has inspired you the most?

**Common Issues and Social Problems** When giving an effect-and-causes speech, think about some of the common issues and social problems that affect people's lives. This can be a good starting point for your speech. It can lead to a more personal topic about a common issue or social problem affecting your own life.

## Vocabulary

A Read the sentences and choose the correct words.

1 Smoking and drinking are two of the leading causes of (cancer / concussions).

2 Money is a major cause of (conflict / contentment) in many marriages. Marriage becomes even more difficult when only one spouse is working.

3 An unstable home life is a leading cause of (academic overachievement / juvenile delinquency).

4 Mandy's mother is an artist, but she (inspired / discouraged) Mandy to follow in her footsteps because she was worried that Mandy wouldn't be able to earn a living in the future.

5 The nature vs. nurture debate asks whether the qualities we possess can be (confused with / attributed to) our genes or our experiences.

6 One of the leading causes of (dementia / insomnia) is using a smartphone before sleeping. If you are going to use your smartphone at night, you should download a blue light filter.

B **Class activity** | Write what you think might be causes of the following effects. When you are finished, share your answers with your classmates.

| Why do people get... | Possible Cause |
| --- | --- |
| insomnia? | *They drink too much caffeine during the day and can't sleep.* |
| cancer? | |
| dementia? | |
| divorced? | |

## Grammar

A Let's learn about *too many* and *too much*.

| too many / too much |
| --- |

More than two alcoholic drinks per day is **too many**. (countable)

If you want to lose weight, you shouldn't eat **too much** bread. Bread has a lot of carbohydrates in it. (uncountable)

B Complete the sentences by writing *many* or *much*.

1 Spending too _____ time looking at a bright screen before bed can affect your sleep.

2 Some family advocacy groups believe there are too _____ divorces in the USA each year.

3 Poverty is one of the reasons there is too _____ crime in our cities.

4 Doctors say even one cigarette a day is too _____.

**An Effect and Its Causes** When giving an effect-and-causes speech, we need to learn some expressions that connect causes to a specific effect. We do this because it is important for the audience to know that our topic is based on a single effect and the possible causes for that effect.

## Language Patterns

A   Let's learn about expressions for describing the causes of a specific effect.

| Effect > Cause | | |
|---|---|---|
| result from<br>be caused by | stem from<br>be produced by | be brought about by<br>be triggered by |

Experts now think that dementia in the elderly can **result from** concussions sustained during childhood or adolescence, poor eating habits, and poor blood circulation.

Many psychologists believe that depression **is triggered by** stress.

B   Practice the expressions in A by using the prompts below.

| Effect | Causes |
|---|---|
| Heart disease... | ...a fatty and sugary diet, smoking, and a lack of exercise. |
| Crime... | ...poverty, poor education, and neglectful parenting. |
| High test scores... | ...a strong support system consisting of teachers and parents, more educational resources, and higher socioeconomic status. |
| Alcoholism... | ...depression, mental illness, and feeling disconnected from friends and family. |

*Heart disease can be caused by a fatty and sugary diet, smoking, and a lack of exercise.*

## Pronunciation 🔊

A   Read and listen to the sentences below. Then practice the pronunciations of the /s/ and /ʃ/ sounds.

| /s/ = "s"  &  /ʃ/ = "sh" |
|---|

Children **s**urely need **s**trong **s**upport **s**ystems.
Depre**ss**ion is a **s**eriou**s** condition.
Extreme **sh**yne**ss** is often a**ss**ociated with low **s**elf-e**s**teem.

B   Listen and practice. Then circle the sound that matches the bold letter.

1 di**s**connected      /s/  or  /ʃ/

2 relation**sh**ip        /s/  or  /ʃ/

3 **s**ugary              /s/  or  /ʃ/

4 **s**moking             /s/  or  /ʃ/

5 concu**ss**ion          /s/  or  /ʃ/

**Main Causes** When giving an effect-and-causes speech, organize the speech so that each main point in the body describes one of the causes. By doing it this way, you can clearly separate the causes you are describing, and it will be easy for the audience to follow.

# Reading 🔊

Read about the main causes for divorce.

 *divorce*

It is not uncommon for newlywed couples to think that the honeymoon stage in their relationships will last forever. They fail to consider the financial responsibilities and parenting realities that may follow their wedding day "I dos." I want to share two of the most common causes of divorce with you. My hope is that you will be able to avoid these problems in your marriages. First, I will talk about attitudes toward money. Then, I will talk about having children. First, let's talk about attitudes toward money. Money is often cited as the number-one reason why married couples fight. During the dating stages of a relationship, a boyfriend isn't responsible for a girlfriend's bills, and vice versa. Once married, however, the spending habits of one person affect the couple as a whole. If the two are responsible with their money, there is little friction with regard to spending and saving. If one person is responsible, but the other person isn't, there can be a lot of conflict. It is extremely important for a young couple planning to marry to make sure that their attitudes regarding money are aligned. If they are not, the couple should delay the wedding until they see eye to eye on the issue. Now, I'd like to talk about couples' attitudes toward having children. It is absolutely imperative that couples talk about whether or not they want to have children before they get married. In many instances, couples agree that they are not going to have children. Then, a few years down the road, one person in the relationship changes his or her mind. The spouse who wants children might even begin to resent his or her partner. That is why it is necessary for couples to speak openly and honestly about their expectations regarding marriage before they decide to tie the knot. If they don't, their marriages could very likely end in divorce.

*tie the knot: slang for "get married"

**Following the Reading** Change the incorrect statements into correct statements.

1 Three important issues facing newly married couples are financial responsibilities and homework.

2 The spending habits of the couple as a whole affect one person.

3 Couples must discuss whether or not they want to have children after the wedding.

4 The writer says it is absolutely imperative that couples speak openly and honestly about their expectations in a marriage before they decide to get divorced.

**Using Charts and Graphs (continued)** As mentioned in Unit 7, charts, graphs, and diagrams can help the audience understand the information in the speech more clearly. Here are four more examples of visuals that are commonly used in speeches and presentations.

A Match the chart, graph, and diagram descriptions with the correct examples. Write the letters in the boxes.

a This kind of diagram is named after its creator. It usually shows two concentric circles overlapping in the center. Each circle represents a single entity, and the overlapping portion of the two circles indicates the parts of the two entities that are the same.

b This kind of chart shows how power is structured in an organization. We sometimes refer to this kind of structure as a hierarchy. It shows how information is delivered from the top of the structure to those in the middle and at the bottom.

c This kind of chart is a combination of a bar chart and a line graph. It can show changes in the volume of a certain entity over a period of time, but it can also show the proportions of the entities as they relate to one another.

d This kind of chart usually presents choices and step-by-step outlines of the consequences of each choice. These charts often use arrows to help viewers navigate a complex series of steps in a process.

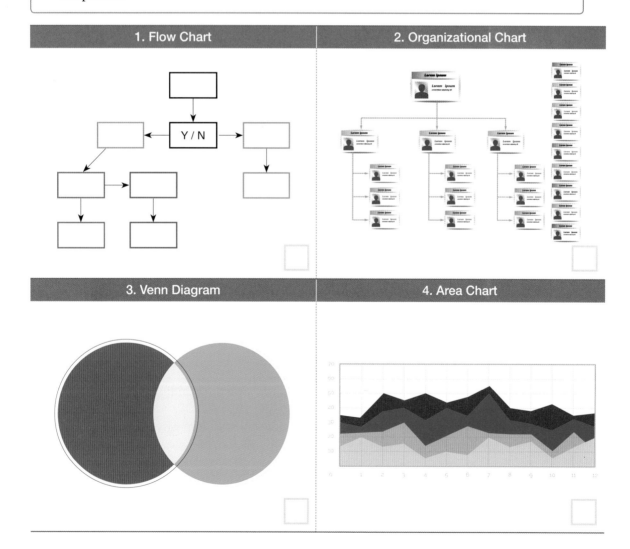

**1. Flow Chart**

Y / N

**2. Organizational Chart**

**3. Venn Diagram**

**4. Area Chart**

B  Complete the speakers' comments by using the information in the charts.

| 1 | Please look at this flow chart with me. When married couples become so unhappy in their relationships that they feel they can no longer stay together, some serious action needs to be considered. There are two avenues they can follow. First, they can choose not to divorce and seek ª _____ . Hopefully, the therapy will result in ᵇ _____ . If the couple decides to divorce, they can split their ᶜ _____ . At this point, they should ᵈ _____ with one another. | |

| 2 | Let's take a look at this area chart. As you can see, third graders with a strong support system and an ª _____ home scored the highest on the weekly reading tests. Those who had a strong support system but lived in a home where there wasn't enough money scored ᵇ _____ than the first group but higher than the ᶜ _____ group. Our last group, those who had a weak support system at home and also lived in a home that was economically unstable scored the lowest. You can see from this ᵈ _____ chart that there are some educational benefits associated with having a strong support system and an economically stable home. | |

**Third Grade Students' Reading Test Scores**

- Strong Support System + Economically Stable
- Strong Support System + Economically Unstable
- Weak Support System + Economically Unstable

1.   2.   3.   4.   5.   6.   7.   8.

| 3 | Let's talk about some of the preventable causes of cancer. The two biggest ones are tobacco use and alcohol use. As you can see from the Venn diagram, the yellow circle represents ª _____ . Smokers are 15 times more likely to develop lung cancer than nonsmokers. The red circle represents ᵇ _____ . Drinking alcohol increases the risk of developing cancers such as esophageal cancer. The overlapping area represents ᶜ _____ . This combination is especially dangerous when considering cancer risks. | |

Smokers and Drinkers

| 4 | I'd like to take a look at a chart that shows the typical hierarchy of a corporation. Now, at the top of the hierarchy are the ª _____ . Beneath the shareholders is the ᵇ _____ . The ᶜ _____ works alongside the board of directors, but he or she is still responsible to the shareholdders. The chief executive officer, or CEO, is next in line after the board of directors and the chairman. Two people report to the CEO. That would be the ᵈ _____ , or COO, and the chief financial officer, or the CFO. | |

### 💧 Common Mistakes  chairman vs. chairperson

chairman: male          chairwoman: female          chairperson: gender neutral (best choice)

# Do It Yourself

**The Informative Speech: An Effect and Its Causes**  Now it is time for you to do it yourself! Use the information you learned in the previous sections in order to create an outline for a speech explaining an effect and its causes.

A   Create an outline for the speech in the spaces below. Choose any effect and its causes (including only two main points is okay). Then use an effect-and-causes organizational pattern to talk about your topic.

### Attention-Getting Opener

Which strategy would you choose for your attention-getting opener?

☐ shocking statistic     ☐ rhetorical question     ☐ anecdote
☐ famous quote     ☐ visual aid     ☐ gimmick

Now, write an attention-getting opener which reveals your topic (an effect) in an interesting way.

_____

_____

Preview of Main Points:

Transition 1:

Main Point 1 (Cause 1):

Transition 2:

Main Point 2 (Cause 2):

Transition 3:

Main Point 3 (Cause 3):

Transition 4:

Summary of Main Points:

### Concluding Remarks

Which strategy would you choose for your concluding remarks?

☐ prediction     ☐ call to action     ☐ complete a story
☐ reference your opening     ☐ answer a question

Now, write your concluding remarks.

_____

B   Give a short speech in which you describe an effect and its causes. Use your notes from A. Try to include a chart or graph in your speech in order to explain any relevant supporting data.

# Checklist

1 Why is it a good idea to start with a list of common issues and societal problems when giving an effect-and-causes speech?

2 What expressions are mentioned in the unit which can be used to link causes to a specific effect?

3 How should we organize the body of an effect-and-causes speech?

4 What are the four types of charts, graphs, or diagrams mentioned in the unit?

## Presentation Tips

### Visual Aids

Make sure your visual aids are in the correct format before you start your speech. You should also make sure that the visuals fit properly on the screen. It is not uncommon for slides to look a little different on a projector screen than they do on your personal computer. It is good practice to arrive at the classroom or boardroom 15 minutes early so that you can test your slides in order to make sure they are working properly. If possible, save your presentation file on the desktop in the room where you are presenting. You never know when a USB drive might malfunction. As the old saying goes, "You are better safe than sorry."

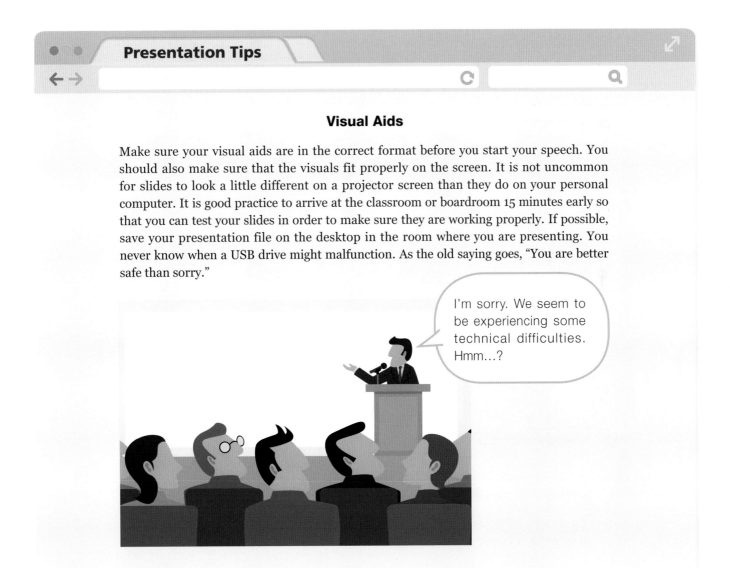

# Group Presentations

## Warm-up

Match the talk types with the correct pictures.

| | | |
|---|---|---|
| Classroom Presentation | Debate | Business Presentation |
| Demonstration | Lecture | Roundtable Discussion |

**Vocabulary for Meetings** It is helpful to learn some common terms related to meetings. These terms are helpful to learn because they are commonly used in many offices around the world. Once you are familiar with these expressions, you can incorporate them into your group's meetings.

## Vocabulary

A Match the words with the correct definitions.

| an agenda | a compromise | collaborate | a deadline | a show of hands | wrap up |

1 _____ : a method for taking a vote by asking those who choose yes (or no) to raise their hands so that their votes can be counted

2 _____ : a list of topics or items to be discussed during a meeting

3 _____ : to cooperate or work together on a project

4 _____ : an agreement between two groups where each side gives the other side something they want

5 _____ : a date and a time when a project or assignment must be completed

6 _____ : to stop or finish up a meeting

B **Pair work | Negotiate a compromise with your partner by using the situations below.**

| Student A: Son/Daughter | Student B: Father/Mother |
|---|---|
| You are a university student, and you live in the school dormitory. Your parents send you an allowance of $200 per month. Only two weeks have passed this month, but you have run out of money. Ask your father for an additional $100. | Your son or daughter is in college and receives a monthly allowance of $200 per month. This month, he or she spent all the money in only two weeks. He or she is now asking for an extra $100. What will you do in this situation? |

A I have a problem, Mom. I spent my monthly allowance in just two weeks.
B I will put some extra money in your account if you promise to wash your father's car.

## Grammar

A Let's learn about the first conditional.

| The First Conditional (If + present simple, ~ will + infinitive) |
|---|

**If** you **lead** this project, the manager **will be** very happy.
**If** the company **reduces** its price by 20%, our firm **will place** more orders.
**If** they don't **meet** us in the library tomorrow, we **won't work** with them.

B Read the dialogue and fill in the blanks by using the correct form of the first conditional.

A Dad, I've got a problem. I already spent my $200 allowance this month.
B But there are two weeks left in the month. It's only October 16!
A ¹_____ you ²_____ another $100 in my account, I ³_____ it next month with money from my part-time job. (put / repay)
B ⁴_____ you ⁵_____ well on your exams this semester, I ⁶_____ you to pay me back. (do / not ask)

# Building Content ❷

**Debating within a Group** When working on a group presentation, you need to discuss and debate the direction of the project. It is important to learn some common expressions for discussion and debate so that you can clearly express your ideas or concerns to the group.

## Language Patterns

A Let's learn some useful expressions you can use during a discussion or a debate.

| Sharing Your Opinion | Agreeing / Disagreeing | Asking for Clarity |
|---|---|---|
| Well, if you ask me... <br> If you want my honest opinion... <br> As far as I'm concerned... | That's right. / That can't be right. <br> I totally agree. / I don't agree at all. <br> I'm convinced that... / I'm not convinced that... | What do you mean? <br> Could you give me an example? <br> What are you trying to say? |

B **Group work** | Check whether you agree or disagree with the hot-button issues in the table. Then share your opinion by using the expressions in A. Let your group members agree, disagree, or ask for clarity regarding your opinions.

| | Hot-Button Issues | Agree | Disagree |
|---|---|---|---|
| 1 | Global climate change is caused by humans. | | |
| 2 | The death penalty is an effective way to reduce crime. | | |
| 3 | Men should get paternity leave from work. | | |
| 4 | We have become too dependent on computers. | | |
| 5 | The government should have some control over our diets. | | |
| 6 | Smoking should be banned in our country. | | |

A If you want my honest opinion, I think climate change is caused by humans.
B What do you mean?
A What I mean is that we burn fossil fuels for energy and that climate change is a result of that activity.
C I'm not convinced that that's true. The Earth has gone through periods of warming and cooling before.

## Pronunciation 🔊

A Read and listen to the sentences below. Then practice the rising and falling intonations related to different kinds of questions.

| Yes/No Questions (rising intonation) | Wh-questions (falling intonation) |
|---|---|
| Are they coming to the meeting? <br> Do you know Kelly? <br> Can they meet us at eight o'clock? | What are you saying? <br> When are they going to finish? <br> Where should we meet? |

B Listen and practice. Be sure to use the correct rising or falling intonation.

1 Do you like giving speeches?

2 When is your business trip?

3 What time does this class finish?

4 Are you kidding me?

**Rules for Successful Group Presentations**  When giving a group presentation, there are some helpful rules your group can follow in order to avoid conflict. By agreeing as a group to adhere to a set of rules, you will waste much less time and improve the likelihood of creating a high-quality presentation.

# Reading 🔊

Read the article about four simple rules for a successful presentation.

## 4 Simple Rules for a Successful Group Presentation

### 1. Communicate

The biggest mistake members of a group make when working together on a presentation is that they stop communicating with one another. Poor communication leads to conflict, and conflict leads to poor results. Members of a group must find a way to communicate with one another respectfully as they work toward a common goal: giving the best group presentation possible.

### 2. Define Your Roles Clearly

If a group is to work efficiently and without conflict, there must be clearly defined roles. On the first day of planning, you should decide who is best suited for each role. We assign roles in a group presentation because it lets each member contribute to the project in a meaningful way. It also utilizes the different talents each member brings to the project.

### 3. Pull Your Weight

Don't let one or two group members do all of the work. Everyone in the group needs to contribute to the project equally. Some roles require more behind-the-scenes work, and others require individuals to be in front of an audience. Both kinds of roles are equally important. If a member of the group is not contributing, you should talk directly with that person. Don't complain about the person to other group members behind his or her back. If the person continues to contribute less than the others, let the group leader handle the situation.

### 4. Listen

Every member of the group deserves to be heard. Sometimes the dominant personalities in a group overshadow those who are shyer and more introverted. By failing to ask for the opinions of quieter individuals, your group could be missing out on some wonderful ideas. A good leader will always be conscious of this fact. He or she will actively seek the opinions of those in the group who have a difficult time speaking up for themselves.

---

*contribute: to give something, such as money or time, in order to accomplish something

**Following the Reading**  Answer the questions.

1  What is the biggest mistake group members make when working together on a presentation?

2  What must happen if a group is to work together efficiently and without conflict?

3  Why do we assign roles in a group presentation?

4  What shouldn't you do if a person is not contributing fairly to a group presentation?

5  What should a good leader always be conscious of?

# Learning How

**Roles in a Group** When giving a group presentation, your group must first decide which roles each person in the group is going to fill. By having defined roles, you will be able to avoid a certain amount of conflict and redundancy. The fairest method for choosing roles is to have a group vote.

A Match the group roles in the box with the correct descriptions.

| Editor | Organizer | IT Specialist | Peacekeeper | Group Leader |

| | |
|---|---|
| 1 | You are in charge of managing the entire group presentation process. You are also responsible for making sure the group stays on task and completes the project on time. |
| 2 | You work closely with the leader to ensure that each member of the group is focused on his or her specific task. Since the leader is busy overseeing the presentation as a whole, you should be focused on the details. |
| 3 | Your job is to make sure that the documents, slides, and visual aids that your group is using in the presentation do not contain any spelling or grammar mistakes. You should also make sure names are spelled correctly. |
| 4 | You are the computer expert in the group. You need to make sure that all documents are saved on a USB drive or in the cloud. You are also responsible for ensuring that the projector works properly on the day of the presentation. |
| 5 | You are responsible for mediating any problems that group members might be having with one another. If there is a problem between group members, your job is to sit down together with them and negotiate a compromise. |

B Rate yourself by using the information in the table. Then choose appropriate roles for each member of your group. Finally, complete the group prewriting exercise.

1 **Rating**

Answer the survey questions by rating yourself from 1 to 5.

| | | | | | | | Total |
|---|---|---|---|---|---|---|---|
| **Group Leader** | | | | | | | |
| 1 | I am comfortable speaking in front of others. | 1 | 2 | 3 | 4 | 5 | / 10 |
| 2 | I possess good leadership qualities. | 1 | 2 | 3 | 4 | 5 | |
| **Organizer** | | | | | | | |
| 3 | I am a very organized person. | 1 | 2 | 3 | 4 | 5 | / 10 |
| 4 | I am good at multitasking. | 1 | 2 | 3 | 4 | 5 | |
| **IT Specialist** | | | | | | | |
| 5 | I am comfortable using computers and computer software. | 1 | 2 | 3 | 4 | 5 | / 10 |
| 6 | I am comfortable using PowerPoint. | 1 | 2 | 3 | 4 | 5 | |
| **Editor** | | | | | | | |
| 7 | I have a good command of English grammar and spelling. | 1 | 2 | 3 | 4 | 5 | / 10 |
| 8 | I find reading and analyzing documents interesting. | 1 | 2 | 3 | 4 | 5 | |
| **Peacekeeper** | | | | | | | |
| 9 | I am good at resolving conflicts among those in a group. | 1 | 2 | 3 | 4 | 5 | / 10 |
| 10 | I have a talent for compromise. | 1 | 2 | 3 | 4 | 5 | |

1 = absolutely not!  2 = not really  3 = no opinion  4 = yes  5 = absolutely yes!

## 2 Choosing Roles

Join four other classmates and choose roles for your group of five. Use your group members' ratings in the survey to help you determine the most appropriate role for each member in the group.

| My Group | |
|---|---|
| Group Leader | |
| Organizer | |
| IT Specialist | |
| Editor | |
| Peacekeeper | |

## 3 Prewriting

Before you begin the writing stage of the group presentation, you must first do the prewriting. Discuss the questions below with your group members and then write your team's answers in the table.

| | Questions | Answers |
|---|---|---|
| 1 | Who is your audience? (classmates, coworkers, customers…) | |
| 2 | What kind of group presentation do you want to give? (classroom presentation, business presentation, debate, roundtable discussion, lecture, demonstration…) | |
| 3 | What is the purpose of your presentation? (inform, persuade, motivate…) | |
| 4 | What is your speech topic? What do you want to talk about in the presentation? | |
| 5 | How will you divide the workload? (Who will write the introduction, body, and conclusion? Who will create visual aids, such as charts and graphs? Who will create the PowerPoint slides? How long will each person speak?) | |
| 6 | Who will do the speaking? Who will deliver the introduction, the body, and the conclusion? | |

## ⓥ Common Mistakes  Debate vs. Discussion

discussion: an exchange of ideas between two or more individuals

debate: an exchange of ideas between two individuals or groups with the purpose of changing the other individual's or group's mind regarding an issue

## Do It Yourself

**Group Presentation: Your Choice of Topic**  Now it is time for you to do it together! Use the information you learned in the previous sections in order to create an outline for your group presentation.

A  Create an outline for your group presentation in the spaces below.

| Attention-Getting Opener |
|---|

Which strategy would you choose for your attention-getting opener?
- ☐ shocking statistic
- ☐ famous quote
- ☐ rhetorical question
- ☐ visual aid
- ☐ anecdote
- ☐ gimmick

Now, write your attention-getting opener.

_____

_____

Preview of Main Points:

Transition 1:

Main Point 1:

Transition 2:

Main Point 2:

Transition 3:

Main Point 3:

Transition 4:

Summary of Main Points:

| Concluding Remarks |
|---|

Which strategy would you choose for your concluding remarks?
- ☐ prediction
- ☐ reference your opening
- ☐ call to action
- ☐ answer a question
- ☐ complete a story

Now, write your concluding remarks.

_____

B  Give a group presentation on a topic of your choice. Use your notes from A.

# Checklist

1 Name three common terms associated with meetings.
2 Why is it important for group members to adhere to a certain set of rules when working as a group?
3 What four rules are mentioned in the unit with regard to working in a group?
4 What are the five roles mentioned in the unit for group presentations?

### Changing from One Speaker to Another in a Group Presentation

When giving a group presentation, there are times when one person is speaking and then must step aside and let another person speak. How can you do this smoothly without causing the flow of the presentation to stop? We can use the following phrases to transition from one speaker to another in the same presentation.

"I'd now like to give the floor to my team member, Melissa."
"Let me hand the microphone over to Melissa."

## Warm-up

Match the historical figures with the correct descriptions. Write the letters in the boxes.

a She was an Albanian-Indian Roman Catholic nun who dedicated her life to helping the poor in India.

b He was an Italian astronomer, physicist, and mathematician. He is considered the father of modern astronomy.

c She was a poor French peasant who eventually became a great military leader. She is famous for leading the French to victory over the English at the Battle of Orleans.

d He was a classical Greek philosopher whose ideas strongly influenced Western philosophy.

e He was a Serbian-American inventor and engineer. His alternating current (AC) electricity supply system challenged Edison's less stable direct current (DC) electricity supply system.

f He was a Chinese philosopher and teacher whose ideas are still influential in modern Asian culture.

1 Confucius

2 Galileo

3 Plato

4 Joan of Arc

5 Nikola Tesla

6 Mother Teresa

**Little-Known Historical Facts** In a speech where you are challenging a common historical belief, you need to provide the audience with reliable facts that support your claim. You should get your information from experts and historians. By using reliable facts, you will gain credibility as a speaker.

## Vocabulary

A **Complete the sentences with the correct words from the word box.**

| chronicles | descent | historians | records | myth | claim |
|---|---|---|---|---|---|

1 Anne Frank's diary _____ her family's experience hiding from the Nazis during the German occupation of the Netherlands in the early 1940s.

2 It is a popular _____ that George Washington, the first president of the United States, never told a lie.

3 The term "Napoleon Complex" refers to the aggression some short people express due to their insecurity with being short; however, _____ from the time show that Napoleon was of average height.

4 Unfortunately, the myth that Abraham Lincoln owned slaves persists even though it has been proven by _____ to be false.

5 Although many attribute the phrase "Let them eat cake" to Marie Antoinette, there is no reliable evidence supporting this _____ .

6 Contrary to common belief, Cleopatra was not actually of Egyptian _____ .

B **Answer the questions about a famous historical figure from your country.**

1 What is the name of a famous historical figure from your country?

2 What is he or she remembered for in your country?

3 Can you think of any popular myths or historical falsehoods surrounding this person?

## Grammar

A **Let's learn about using apostrophes to show possession.**

| Possessive ('s) |
|---|
| Anne Frank**'s** diary has been published in hundreds of languages. (Anne Frank's diary = her diary) <br> The slaves followed Harriet Tubman**'s** path to freedom. (Harriet Tubman's path to freedom = her path to freedom) <br> Confucius**'s** teachings encourage respect for the society's elders. (Confucius's teachings = his teachings) |

B **Complete the sentences with the correct possessives.**

1 _____ *A People's History* is my favorite history book. (Howard Zinn)

2 _____ *Mona Lisa* is located in the Louvre in Paris. (Leonardo da Vinci)

3 I found _____ autobiography very interesting. (Quincy Jones)

**Expressing Opposition to a Viewpoint** When challenging a common belief about history, you should begin your argument by expressing opposition to the commonly held belief. Once you have done this, you can provide the audience with the real history of the event based on your research and experts' opinions.

## Language Patterns

A Let's learn how to express opposition to a viewpoint.

| Expressing Opposition |
|---|
| Although some people believe ~, I don't agree with this viewpoint. |
| Even though some people think ~, I have an opposing view. |
| Despite the fact that some people believe ~, I disagree with this view. |
| In spite of the fact that some people think ~, I'd like to share an opposing viewpoint. |
| Contrary to common belief, I think... / Contrary to common belief, I don't think... |

B Read the common myths in the table. Then express opposition to the viewpoints by using the expressions in A.

| | Historical Falsehoods |
|---|---|
| 1 | An apple fell on Newton's head, giving him his idea for the law of gravity. |
| 2 | Marie Antoinette said, "Let them eat cake," to the starving people of France. |
| 3 | Captain James Cook discovered Australia. |
| 4 | Columbus proved that the Earth was round. |
| 5 | Shakespeare wrote the play *Hamlet*. |

*Although some people believe an apple fell on Newton's head, giving him his idea for the law of gravity, I don't agree with this viewpoint.*

## Pronunciation 🔊

A Read and listen to the words below. Then practice the pronunciations of the /I/ and /i/ sounds.

| /I/ | /i/ |
|---|---|
| win | wean |
| pick | peak |
| live | leave |
| his | he's |

B Listen and practice. Be careful when pronouncing the /I/ and /i/ sounds.

1 It was a big win for the team.

2 More in-depth research is necessary.

3 Don't leave until you speak to Tim.

4 He grew up in Sweden.

5 Peace is possible if the two countries continue to meet.

**Challenging a Common Belief** If the purpose of your speech is to challenge a common historical belief, you must first address the common belief in the introduction. Then, you should make a persuasive claim that counters the incorrect historical event and provide supporting evidence in the body that supports your claim.

# Reading 🔊

A Read the article challenging common beliefs about Christopher Columbus.

Elementary school teachers around the world love to tell the Christopher Columbus story to their students. In the story, Columbus sets sail to the Americas in order to prove to ignorant Europeans that the Earth is round. Does this version of the story sound familiar to you? It is the version that I grew up believing. Although some people still believe this version of the story is true, I'd like to share an opposing viewpoint. I'm going to tell you the true story of Columbus's voyage to the Americas. First, I'm going to tell you what Europeans really believed about the Earth in 1492. Then, I'm going to tell you what the real purpose of Columbus's voyage was.

First, let me talk about what Europeans would have thought about a round Earth in 1492. It's true that for a brief time during the Middle Ages, illiterate and uneducated Europeans believed the Earth was flat. However, by the year 1500, the idea that the Earth was round was considered common knowledge in Europe. According to Michael Wenkart, the author of *The 50 Greatest Events in the History of Humankind*, several books were written between 1200 and 1500 that discussed the Earth's shape as round. One example, *The Sphere*, was written in the early 1200s and was required reading at European universities in the 1300s and beyond. So there's no doubt that educated elites during Columbus's time believed the Earth was round. Eventually, these ideas which were considered true by the rich and powerful became common knowledge among Europe's peasantry as well.

Now, let's talk about Columbus's real purpose. Columbus was not sailing west to prove that the Earth was round; however, he was looking for a shorter trade route to China and India. Columbus was convinced that Asia was much closer than most people at his time thought. He believed a shorter trade route was possible by going west instead of the traditional trade route, which was to the south.

*elites: a class of people who are considered superior or special for various reasons
*peasantry: poor farmers and farm laborers of low social status

**Following the Reading** Read the statements and mark True or False.

1 Some people believe Columbus sailed west to prove that the Earth was flat. [True / False]

2 *The Sphere* was required reading at European universities in the 1300s. [True / False]

3 Educated elites in Europe would have believed that the Earth was round during Columbus's time.
[True / False]

4 Columbus thought a western route to China and India was longer than a southern route. [True / False]

B Can you think of any historical inaccuracies associated with your country's historical figures? What myths have you been told about historical figures from your country?

## Learning How

**Citing Sources** When giving a speech which challenges a commonly held view about a historical event, you need to conduct research. In order to prove to the audience that the ideas in the speech are not only your ideas but also the ideas of experts and historians, you should cite your sources.

A  Match the source types with the correct citations.

a  Direct Quotation: *(famous person) said, "(quotation)."*

b  Book: *According to (author's name), the author of (book title)...*

c  Newspaper/Magazine: *On (date, year), (newspaper/magazine's name) explained that...*

d  Website: *According to the website (website URL), it is...*

e  Interviews/lectures/talks: *In a/an interview/lecture/talk at (location) on (date, year), (speaker's name) said...*

(1) Upon taking his first step on the moon, Neil Armstrong said, "That's one small step for a man; one giant leap for mankind."

(2) According to the website www.realhistory.com, it is true that innocent women thought to be witches were killed during the Salem Witch Trials of 1692; however, none of the so-called witches was burned at the stake. The preferred method of execution was hanging.

(3) In a lecture at Capital City University on January 12, Dr. Frank Bachman said, "Many people mistakenly believe that Napoleon and his army used the nose of the Egyptian Sphinx as a practice target for cannon fire. We know this is false because the Sphinx can be seen without its nose in a sketch done thirty years before Napoleon was born."

(4) According to Cecil Bryant, the author of *Earth from Space*, contrary to popular belief, the Great Wall of China is not visible from space.

(5) On November 14, 2006, the *Capital City Times* explained that contrary to the storyline in the popular film *300*, there were far more than *300* soldiers preventing the Persian army from advancing on the Spartan soldiers during the Battle of Thermopylae.

B  Use the sources in order to make citations. Use the citation strategies in A.

1

**Lecturer**: Miriam De Silva, Historian of Ancient Greek Literature and Arts

**Excerpt from lecture at Eastern University on October 31, 2018**: When we think about ancient Grecian sculptures, we picture smooth porcelain-colored gods and goddesses. At the time, though, these statues were painted in bright, beautiful colors.

2

Date: August 3, 2018

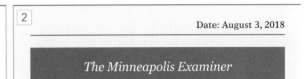

*The Minneapolis Examiner*

Despite the fact that many believe Richard Nixon was forced from the office of the United States presidency soon after the Watergate scandal broke, in reality, it took several years for the impeachment process to proceed.

3

www.harshhistory.com

Even though many people still believe that vomitoriums in ancient Rome were rooms where wealthy Roman men and women ate and drank until they vomited, the truth is that a vomitorium was a large entranceway in a stadium where crowds of people entered and exited the stadium.

4

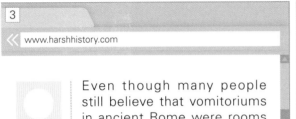

It was true that life expectancy in the Middle Ages was lower than today; however, much of it was due to the high infant mortality rate at the time.
- Ron West PhD

5

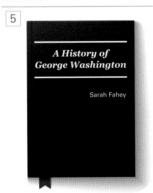

*A History of George Washington*

Sarah Fahey

It's a myth that George Washington had wooden teeth. His false teeth were probably made of a combination of gold, ivory, and animal teeth, which were materials commonly used for such purposes at the time.

🛸 **Common Mistakes** **MD vs. PhD**

MD = medical doctor                PhD = doctor of philosophy

# Do It Yourself

**The Persuasive Speech: Challenge a Common Historical Belief** Now it is time for you to do it yourself! Use the information you learned in the previous sections in order to create an outline for a speech challenging a common historical belief.

A   Create an outline for the speech in the spaces below. Prepare a speech where you challenge a commonly held belief about history. Remember to cite your sources in the speech.

| Attention-Getting Opener |
| --- |

Which strategy would you choose for your attention-getting opener?

☐ shocking statistic       ☐ rhetorical question       ☐ anecdote
☐ famous quote       ☐ visual aid       ☐ gimmick

Now, write an attention-getting opener.

Write Your Persuasive Claim:

Preview of Main Points:

Transition 1:

Main Point 1 (Supporting Evidence 1):

Transition 2:

Main Point 2 (Supporting Evidence 2):

Transition 3:

Main Point 3 (Supporting Evidence 3):

Transition 4:

Summary of Main Points:

| Concluding Remarks |
| --- |

Which strategy would you choose for your concluding remarks?

☐ prediction       ☐ call to action       ☐ complete a story
☐ reference your opening       ☐ answer a question

Now, write your concluding remarks.

B   Give a short speech in which you challenge an incorrect historical belief. Use your notes from A.

# Checklist

1 Why should you get your facts from historians or other experts?

2 When challenging a common belief, how should you begin your argument?

3 What must the speaker be sure to include in the body of a speech which challenges a commonly held belief?

4 How can you prove you have done proper research for a speech?

**Presentation Tips**

### Ethos, Pathos, and Logos

In Western argumentation, there are three key strategies speakers can use to persuade listeners: **ethos**, **pathos**, and **logos**. **Ethos** is an appeal to the audience's sense of ethics. Ethos relies heavily on the credibility of the speaker and the sources he or she uses in the speech. **Pathos** is an appeal to the audience's emotions. Pathos requires a certain level of passion for the topic, evidenced in the speaker's voice. Storytelling is another effective way to connect with an audience emotionally. **Logos** is an appeal to the audience's sense of logic. Logos requires the use of reason and facts to make a persuasive argument.

# Advertising

## Warm-up

A  Write the correct types of advertising mediums under the pictures.

| | | |
|---|---|---|
| television commercial | radio spot | billboard |
| flier | magazine/newspaper ad | Internet ad |

B  Which kinds of advertisements do you think are the most effective and the least effective?

**Describing a Product** When trying to persuade an audience to buy a specific product, you need to describe it in an attractive way. You should try to avoid common adjectives such as *good* or *nice*. Use descriptive language that makes the product look more enticing to the audience.

## Vocabulary

A   Complete the comments by using the words in the word box.

| bargain | satisfaction guaranteed | compact | unique | durable | five-star |
|---|---|---|---|---|---|

1 Our products are _____ or your money back!

2 No other hiking boots are as _____ as Epic Climbz hiking boots. They'll last a lifetime!

3 Zorbo's stretchy jeans are like no other product on the market. Our _____ jeans will make you feel stylish and comfortable.

4 If you spend one night at our _____ hotel, you'll never go back to a regular hotel again!

5 All Antonio's pizzas are 50% off on the last day of the month. It's an amazing _____!

6 Suntao Motors Company's newest car is _____ and fuel efficient. It's fun to drive, and because of its size, it can fit into any parking space.

B   Think of items that you own that possess the qualities of the words in the left column. Then write the names of the products in the right column.

| Description | Product Type |
|---|---|
| durable | |
| unique | |
| compact | |
| bargain | |

## Grammar

A   Let's learn about the first conditional with various modal auxiliary verbs.

| If Clause (If + sub. + verb) + Main Clause (sub. + modal + verb) |
|---|

**If** you want to purchase a pair of Sunlife sunglasses, you **must** order them at www.sunlife.com. It's the only platform available.

**If** you are tired of buying new hiking boots every two years, you **should** purchase a pair of Epic Climbz boots. They're fantastic!

**If** you call our operators now, you **can** save 20% on your first purchase!

B   Complete the sentences by using the appropriate modal auxiliary verbs.

1 If you want to look good, you _____ buy a pair of Cool Ray Sunglasses. They look cool!

2 If we want to get to Brooklyn, we _____ cross the Brooklyn Bridge. There's no other option.

3 If you order now, you _____ choose between three colors: black, red, and white.

# Building Content ❷

**Visualizing the Future** To sell a product to an audience, you must help the listeners imagine a future where they have purchased and used your product. Make them realize that life without your product is worse than life with it. You must use language that paints a mental picture of this ideal future.

## Language Patterns

A  Let's learn some expressions for visualizing the future.

| Visualizing the Future |
| --- |
| Picture a future where... |
| Imagine a future where... |
| Picture a time when... |
| Imagine a time when... |
| Think about what it will be like when... |
| Imagine what it will be like when... |
| Imagine how nice it'll be when... |
| Just think about how nice it'll be when... |

B  **Speaking** | **Make sentences that paint a visual picture of the products in the table by using the expressions in A.**

| | Product Types |
| --- | --- |
| 1 | Five-Star Hotel in Hawaii |
| 2 | 65-Inch Flat-Screen Television |
| 3 | New Dress / New Suit |
| 4 | King-Sized Bed |
| 5 | Luxury Car |
| 6 | Memory Foam Mattress |

*Imagine a future where you are relaxing on a beach in Hawaii with your loved one.*

## Pronunciation 🔊

A  **Read and listen to the sentences below. Then practice the pronunciations of *It'll* and *What'll*.**

| It'll = /Idəl/ | What'll = /wədəl/ |
| --- | --- |
| Imagine what **it'll** be like when you are lying on the beach in Thailand. | **What'll** people say when they see your new luxury car? |

B  **Listen and practice. Be careful when pronouncing *It'll* and *What'll*.**

1  A  **What'll** our classmates say when they see my new haircut?
    B  They'll be shocked. It's really short now.

2  A  Just think how nice **it'll** be when we get our new 65-inch flat-screen television.
    B  I can't wait. **It'll** be like watching a movie in the theater, except **it'll** be in our living room.

**Putting It All Together** If your claim to the audience is that their lives will be better if they purchase your product, then you must provide reasons and examples that support this claim. Remember to use interesting descriptive language to help them visualize a future where they have the item.

# Reading 🔊

Read about the company's ergonomic office chair.

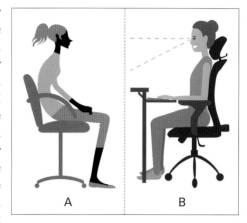

80% of us will experience lower back pain at some point in our lives. In the modern workplace, we spend much of our time sitting. Many of the chairs we sit on do not provide enough back support. What if I told you that you could still sit at your desk all day but not feel any pain? Today, I'm going to tell you why you need the Erickson Ergonomic Office Chair. First, I will tell you how it works. Then, I will tell you what your life could be like with this chair. Finally, I'll tell you how you can purchase this chair for yourself. First, let me describe the chair for you. The Erickson Ergonomic Office Chair has a unique ergonomic design that imitates the natural curvature of the spine. Take a look at image A. You can see that the woman in the picture is hunched over. Her chair does not offer any back support. Now look at the chair in image B. Notice how it supports the woman's lower back. It's helping her maintain a much healthier posture for her spine. The woman's shoulders are back, her spine is upright, and she appears to be much more comfortable. Now, I'd like you to imagine a future without any back pain. Imagine a time when you are working at your desk all day, but at the end of the day, you feel great. In fact, after work, you feel so good that you decide to play tennis with your friends or take your dog for a long walk. All of this is possible if you start using the Erickson Ergonomic Office Chair. Finally, I'd like to talk to you about the price. The Erickson Ergonomic Office Chair costs $99.99. This chair is no more expensive than your typical office chair. Why not spend the same money and live a life without back pain? Visit the Erickson website at www.ericksonergo.com and browse our various styles and colors of chairs. Don't live in pain any longer!

*curvature: being curved; a degree of curve in something

**Following the Reading**   Answer the questions.

1 Why do so many people experience lower back pain in their lifetimes?

2 Why are Erickson's ergonomic chairs unique?

3 Is it healthier to sit hunched over or with a straight spine and your shoulders back?

4 What kind of future does the writer ask us to imagine?

5 Why is Erickson's Ergonomic Office Chair a great bargain?

**Monroe's Motivated Sequence**  Alan H. Monroe was a university professor at Purdue University in the United States. He developed a five-step method of persuasion that is still taught at schools, universities, and businesses all around the world. His method of persuasion has proven to be very effective.

A  Match the steps with the correct descriptions.

> a  Step 1: Grab the Attention of Your Listeners
>
> b  Step 2: Establish a Need
>
> c  Step 3: Satisfy the Need
>
> d  Step 4: Visualize the Future
>
> e  Step 5: Encourage the Listeners to Take Action

(1) In this step, you are going to offer a solution to the problem that you have made the audience aware of. This is the core of your speech. Use facts, statistics, and other evidence you have collected during the research stage of the speech preparation process. You do this in order to convince the audience that your solution to the problem is the best choice. ☐

(2) In this step, you can help the audience imagine what the world will look like if they accept your solution. Paint a positive mental picture for the listener. You can also paint a dark picture of the future, one where your solution is not adopted and the problem persists or worsens. ☐

(3) This step is sometimes referred to as the hook. You want the audience to sit up and to take notice. You can use a shocking statistic, a humorous story, a visual aid, or something similar. This step in Monroe's Motivated Sequence should be included in all speeches, both informative and persuasive. ☐

(4) In this step, you should give the audience specific things that they can do to actively solve this problem. You might ask them to visit a website or to read a book. It might be information about where to buy a certain product. If your speech is successful, your motivational message will transform itself into some form of action by the audience. ☐

(5) In this step, the speaker should convince the audience that there's a problem that needs to be solved. Use supporting details, reasons, and evidence to support your claim. Don't offer solutions at this stage. Instead, let the audience sit for a moment in the knowledge that there's a problem that needs fixing. Build anticipation. ☐

B  Match the steps with the correct slides.

| | | |
|---|---|---|
| 1 | Step 1: Grab the Attention of Your Listeners | |
| 2 | Step 2: Establish a Need | |
| 3 | Step 3: Satisfy the Need | |
| 4 | Step 4: Visualize the Future | |
| 5 | Step 5: Encourage the Listeners to Take Action | |

**a**
- 1 out of 3 people not getting enough sleep
- Back pain result of old mattresses
- Need 7 hours of sleep per night

**b**
- Memory foam contours to shape of body
- Cools body when hot
- Warms body when cold
- Supports spine
- Get great sleep
- Hypoallergenic

**c**
- Purchase at www.sleeptech. com
- Enter special promo code 559 and get a 10% discount

**d**
*Does this happen to you?*

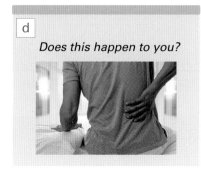

**e**
*Imagine a future with...*
- no back pain in the morning
- amazing sleep
- the most comfortable mattress in the world

C  Imagine you have been asked to make a sales pitch for an existing product. Choose any existing product and answer the questions in the table below by using Monroe's Motivated Sequence.

| | | |
|---|---|---|
| 1 | Who is your audience? | |
| 2 | What problem or need does your product address? | |
| 3 | Do you think your audience will identify with the problem? If yes, continue to question 4. If not, go back to question 2. | |
| 4 | How will your product satisfy the listeners' needs? | |
| 5 | What does a future with your product look like? | |

🐱 **Common Mistakes  Capitalization**

Purdue University (correct)          university (correct)          University (incorrect)

## Do It Yourself

**The Persuasive Speech: Give a Short Sales Pitch for an Existing Product** Now it is time for you to do it yourself! Use the information you learned in the previous sections in order to create an outline for a speech giving a short sales pitch for an existing product.

A Create an outline for the speech in the spaces below. Choose a product you would like to advertise to the class. Then use Monroe's Motivated Sequence to organize your speech.

### Step 1: Attention-Getting Opener

Which strategy would you choose for your attention-getting opener?

☐ shocking statistic    ☐ rhetorical question    ☐ anecdote
☐ famous quote          ☐ visual aid             ☐ gimmick

Now, write your attention-getting opener.

### Step 2: Establish a Need

### Step 3: Satisfy the Need

### Step 4: Visualize the Future

### Step 5: Encourage Your Listeners to Take Action

B Give a short speech in which you try to persuade the audience to buy a specific product by using Monroe's Motivated Sequence to formulate your argument. Use your notes from A.

# Checklist

1 Why should we avoid using common adjectives when persuading an audience to buy a product?

2 To sell a product to an audience, what must you make them realize?

3 What is Monroe's Motivated Sequence?

4 What are the steps in Monroe's Motivated Sequence?

**Presentation Tips**

## Voice Register

We use different voice registers to indicate changing moods and feelings. This is especially true for English speakers. Unlike tonal languages, English is heavily dependent on syntax (grammar) for meaning. We adjust the register of our voices to indicate a spectrum of emotions. For example, if a person were expressing frustration over the recent purchase of an item that wasn't working properly, his or her voice would rise to a higher pitch than normal. This would indicate his or her frustration or annoyance with the product. Pathos is a persuasive speaking strategy that uses emotions as a way to get the audience to agree with an argument. In order to make an emotional appeal to an English-speaking audience, we must use different vocal registers. If a speaker is giving a speech about a serious issue, his or her voice might drop to a lower register. This tells the audience that he or she would like everyone in the room to listen intently and take the information being shared seriously. By using different voice registers, we more effectively capture the interest of the audience and show them that we care about the position we are arguing for.

# Making a Change

## Warm-up

A Look at the before and after photos. Then match the comments with the correct picture pairs.

> a Since I had already graduated from university, my parents thought it was time I found my own place. They wanted me to move out of their home and into my own apartment.
>
> b All I did was play games all day, but I wasn't learning anything. I needed to get an education.
>
> c I knew what my dream job was, but I was wasting my life at a boring office job. I'd had enough!
>
> d I was sick of living a sedentary lifestyle. I needed to make a change!

B Do you have anything you would like to change about your life? If so, what is it?

**Then and Now** In a speech about changing a behavior, you can talk about your own experiences. Talk about how you used to behave and how you have changed. You can show that change is possible.

## Vocabulary

A Read the sentences and choose the correct words.

1 Petra thinks working as a barista in a café is (a waste of / a good use of) her talent. She's going to start performing with bands on weekends in the hope of starting a singing career.

2 Junyoung decided to (play it safe / take a chance) by quitting his office job and by freelancing as a graphic designer.

3 Playing video games at the arcade with friends was fun, but it was (fruitful / unproductive). Now I'm a manager at the arcade, and I really enjoy working there!

4 The doctor told Shinzo that his (sedentary / energetic) lifestyle would eventually cause him some serious health problems, so he began working out at the gym three times a week.

5 Lina had (assurances / doubts) she would find a job in advertising, but after three months of intense searching, she finally landed a job at a good firm.

B Imagine you are the people in the picture sets. Then by using the picture cues, make true sentences describing how you used to be and how you are now.

*I used to be sedentary, but now I'm active. I go hiking in the mountains regularly.*

## Grammar

A Let's learn about the expression "used to."

| (past habits, attitudes, and behaviors) |
| --- |
| April **used to** be sedentary, but now she's extremely active.<br>Sumin **used to** think becoming an actress was impossible, but now she believes she can do it.<br>John and Mindy **used to** live in fear, but now they aren't afraid to take chances. |

B Change the sentences into one by using the expression "used to."

1 I was unmotivated. Now, I'm motivated.

2 Chen was unemployed. Now, he has a job.

3 Jim wasted his time. Now, he's productive.

4 Wendy lived alone. Now, she has a roommate.

**Start Now or Stop Now** In a speech where the purpose is to get the audience to start or stop a specific behavior, it is useful to use strong commanding language because your purpose is to motivate the listeners.

## Language Patterns

A  Let's learn some expressions for suggesting that a person start or stop doing something now.

| Start Now! / Stop Now! | |
|---|---|
| Wait no more! | Don't wait anymore! |
| Wait no longer! | Don't wait any longer! |
| Delay no further! | Don't delay any further! |
| Procrastinate no longer! | Don't procrastinate any longer! |

B  **Pair work** | Take turns making excuses from the table below. Comment on the excuses by using the expressions in A. Include reasons why the other person's excuses are poor.

| 1 | I'd like to lose five kilograms, but I don't want to join a gym. |
|---|---|
| 2 | I want to get a new job in a different industry, but I'm scared. |
| 3 | I'm thinking about learning Korean, but I've heard it's kind of hard. |
| 4 | I'd like to find a romantic partner, but I hate going out. |
| 5 | I'd like to write a novel, but I don't have any good ideas. |
| 6 | I want to learn a musical instrument, but I don't have enough money for lessons. |

A I'd like to lose five kilograms, but I don't want to go to a gym.

B Don't procrastinate any longer! You don't need a gym membership to lose five kilograms. There are hundreds of home workouts online that you can do in your home for free.

## Pronunciation 🔊

A  Read and listen to the sentences below. Then practice the pronunciations of *but I...*, *and I...*, and *or I...*

| but I = /bədal/   and I = /endal/   or I = /oʊral/ |
|---|

I'd like to lose five kilograms, **but I** don't want to join a gym.
My brother **and I** want to visit the Grand Canyon.
Meet me this weekend, **or I** am going to find a new partner for the project.

B  Listen and practice. Be careful when pronouncing *but I...*, *and I...*, and *or I...*

1 I want to learn English, **but I** don't like studying.

2 My mother **and I** have dark brown hair. However, my father **and I** have blue eyes.

3 I will either start the project tonight, **or I** will wait until Monday.

**Follow Your Bliss** When giving a speech about changing a behavior, you can use a real person from your own life as an example of someone who has succeeded. It can inspire audience members to change.

## Reading 🔊

A  **Read about following your professional dream.**

My best friend Angela landed a high-paying office job at a large company. But when we would talk, I could hear a hint of sadness in her voice. I want to tell you about the importance of following your professional dream. First, I will discuss why it is necessary to pursue your dream. Then, I will talk about how you can accomplish it. Finally, I will ask you to visualize your life in a career that satisfies your soul.

First, let's talk about the necessity of following your professional dream. There are a lot of people who work in jobs that they don't enjoy. They do them only to pay the bills. Author and professor Joseph Campbell encouraged his students to follow their bliss. He defined bliss as the career path that not only satisfied your mind but also your soul. He believed that when you followed your bliss, professional doors opened because you met likeminded individuals who shared the same passions.

The longer you wait to change careers, the more difficult it will become. Ask yourself what your professional dream is. Then, set a long-term goal. After that, make a series of short-term goals that will help you achieve your long-term goal. The satisfaction you get by meeting your short-term goals will give you the motivation needed to reach your long-term goal.

It's important to visualize your dream. Imagine a future where you have reached your long-term goal. If your dream is to work in the performing arts, think about how incredible it would feel to finally perform on a stage in front of a crowd. It wouldn't matter if there were ten people or ten thousand people in the audience because you would be doing what you love.

At the beginning of the speech, I told you about Angela. Her true dream was to become a chef. Last week, she finished her last day at her company. She starts culinary school next month. She's going to learn to become a chef. She is following her bliss!

**Following the Reading**  **Answer the questions.**

1  What could the author hear in her friend's voice when they talked?

2  How did Joseph Campbell define bliss?

3  What advice does the author give with regard to achieving a long-term goal? Why does the author recommend this strategy?

4  What was Angela's true passion in life?

B  **Are you currently doing your dream job? If so, how did you find your dream job? If not, what would you like to be doing for a living?**

**A Call to Action** In a speech where the purpose of the talk is to change a behavior, the concluding remarks should be a call to action. A call to action is a plea to the audience to actually do something with the information they have learned. There are four elements to an effective call to action.

A   Write the correct elements from the box in the table.

Make your call to action concise and clear.    Make your call to action easy to perform.

Make the urgency of the situation clear.    Make sure you know your audience.

| 1 | 2 |
| --- | --- |
| One of the key elements of making an effective call to action is the ability to convince the audience that that action needs to be taken immediately. To do this effectively, you need to use language that appeals to the audience's emotions. In persuasive argumentation, we call this pathos. Create a burning desire in the audience to make a change now. Make the audience believe that change can wait no longer. | A good call to action is brief and well defined. A long, drawn-out call to action will cause the audience to lose interest in the talk. In addition, a speech with concluding remarks that are too long leaves the audience feeling like the speech is out of balance as a whole. Begin your concluding remarks by stating your call to action in one precise sentence. This will eliminate any misunderstanding regarding what you are asking your listeners to do. Give the audience a direct message that they can act on. |

| 3 | 4 |
| --- | --- |
| This step requires you to do a little research before you prepare your concluding remarks. You must know what kind of group you are asking to take action. Your messaging might be different if you are talking to university students as opposed to businesspeople. By understanding what motivates your listeners and what concerns are most pressing in their lives, you can customize your concluding remarks and make sure your call to action makes the greatest possible impact. | In an effective call to action, the audience is given instructions which are easy to perform. These instructions could include signing a petition, making a phone call, or visiting a website. The actions you are requesting must not be too complicated or labor-intensive. By adding too many steps to the process, you are reducing the chances that the audience members will actually do what you are asking of them. |

Visit the World Cancer Research Fund website today to make a donation. The web address is www.wcr...

B  Match each call to action with the correct persuasive claim.

> a  Sign up for the club after my talk. You'll make new friends and improve your English skills!
>
> b  Visit the website www.wcrf.org and make a donation. You'll save lives!
>
> c  We need to reduce our carbon footprint, so put the car key back on the shelf and pull out your bus or train pass. We all must do our part.
>
> d  Check the batteries in your alarms at least once a month. Doing that could save lives.
>
> e  Visit your local government office today and ask for a donor's form. It's that simple.
>
> f  Contact Barbara in HR at extension 5522 and sign up for our ride-sharing service. You'll save money and help the environment!

| | Persuasive Claim | Call to Action |
|---|---|---|
| 1 | You should donate money to the World Cancer Research Fund. | |

| | Persuasive Claim | Call to Action |
|---|---|---|
| 2 | Becoming an organ donor is one of the most precious gifts you can give. | |

| | Persuasive Claim | Call to Action |
|---|---|---|
| 3 | Everyone should be using public transportation these days. | |

| | Persuasive Claim | Call to Action |
|---|---|---|
| 4 | Join the English club at school today! | |

| | Persuasive Claim | Call to Action |
|---|---|---|
| 5 | Check the smoke alarms in your house every month. | |

| | Persuasive Claim | Call to Action |
|---|---|---|
| 6 | Don't drive to work alone. Join a carpool! | |

**Common Mistakes  once, twice, three times**

once a month (correct)          one time a month (correct)          once time a month (incorrect)

once, twice, thrice (less common usage)          once, twice, three times (common usage)

## Do It Yourself

**The Persuasive Speech: Give a Speech Encouraging the Audience to Make a Change in Their Lives** Now it is time for you to do it yourself! Use the information you learned in the previous sections in order to create an outline for a speech encouraging the audience to make a change in their lives.

A  Create an outline for the speech in the spaces below. Use Monroe's Motivated Sequence to organize your speech. Make your concluding remarks a call to action.

### Step 1: Attention-Getting Opener

Which strategy would you choose for your attention-getting opener?

☐ shocking statistic ☐ rhetorical question ☐ anecdote
☐ famous quote ☐ visual aid ☐ gimmick

Now, write your attention-getting opener.

### Step 2: Establish a Need

### Step 3: Satisfy the Need

### Step 4: Visualize the Future

### Step 5: Encourage Your Listeners to Take Action

B  Give a short speech in which you encourage your classmates to make a change in their lives. Use your notes from A.

# Checklist

1 In a speech where the purpose is to change a behavior, why is it a good idea to use strong commanding language?

2 What is the benefit of using a real person from your own life as an example in a speech about changing a behavior?

3 Which strategy should you use for the concluding remarks of a speech in which the purpose is to change a behavior?

4 What are the four elements to an effective call to action?

**Presentation Tips**

### Choosing a Purpose

There are three main purposes for speaking persuasively. First, you can try to change people's **opinions** about a specific topic. By changing an opinion, you are trying to convince an audience that something that was thought to be good is actually bad, or vice versa. Opinions can never be proven because they are based on people's preferences. Secondly, you can try to change a **belief**. In this case, you are trying to convince an audience that something which many people thought was true is actually false, or vice versa. In this case, you must provide facts, evidence, and experts' opinions to support your claim. Lastly, you can try to change people's **behaviors**. In this case, you want them to stop a bad or unhealthy behavior and start a positive or healthy one. You must provide compelling reasons and realistic solutions as you try to convince them that a behavioral change is in their best interest.

# Childhood Memories

Unit **1**

## Building Content ❶

p.9

### Vocabulary

A

1 remarkable          2 silly
3 picturesque         4 frightening
5 a nerve-racking

### Grammar

B

1 moved              2 saw
3 rode               4 wanted
5 bought             6 stopped

## Building Content ❸

p.11

### Reading

**Following the Reading**

1 They went to Niagara Falls.
2 He was bored during the trip.
3 He was 13 years old.
4 It was more painful because she had known Buddy for his entire life.
5 They ordered pizza and watched scary movies.
6 They talk about the fun times they had in junior high school.

## Learning How

p.12

A

1 Orlando
2 Disney characters
3 sick
4 Disney World
5 Cinderella's castle
6 Space Mountain
7 twelve
8 ferry
9 took pictures
10 Big Thunder

B

(Example Answer)

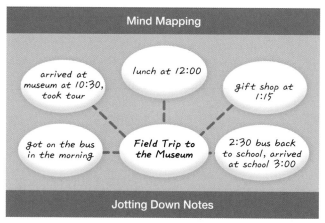

**Mind Mapping**

- arrived at museum at 10:30, took tour
- lunch at 12:00
- gift shop at 1:15
- got on the bus in the morning
- Field Trip to the Museum
- 2:30 bus back to school, arrived at school 3:00

**Jotting Down Notes**

### Field Trip to the Museum

- got on the bus at 9:45 a.m.
- arrived at the museum at 10:30 and took a tour
- had lunch at 12:00
- visited museum gift shop at 1:15
- got on the bus to return to school at 2:30
- arrived at school at 3:00

**Freewritng**

Everyone got on the bus in the morning at 9:30. John, my classmate was late that day. He almost missed the bus to the museum. We arrived at the museum at 10:30 and immediately took a tour of the museum. Our guide was young, in her 20s I think. She was really good at her job. The tour was very informative. I especially liked the Renaissance era artwork. At noon, we had lunch. My mom packed a peanut butter and jelly sandwich for me. I hate peanut butter and jelly sandwiches. I gave the sandwich to my friend, and in return, he let me drink half of his soda. After lunch, we went to the gift shop. My mother had given me five dollars, but I only spent one dollar on a silly key chain. I kept the other four dollars. I told my mom that the key chain cost $5.00. She was shocked at the price of the key chain. We boarded the bus back to school at 2:30. It took about 30 minutes to get back. We arrived at the school at 3:00. Everyone got off the bus and went home. My friends and I didn't go home though. We went to the arcade to play video games. I had an extra $4.00 that I needed to spend!

## Checklist

p.15

1 It can tell the audience how you felt.
2 A good story requires a beginning, a middle, and an ending.

3 Your recollection of the events that occurred and the emotions that you felt at the time are two factors that will help create an interesting narrative.
4 Brainstorming should be the first step in the speech-writing process.
5 Mind mapping, jotting down notes, and freewriting are mentioned in the unit.

## Success

### Building Content ❶
p.17

#### Vocabulary
A

| | | |
|---|---|---|
| 1 d | 2 c | 3 a |
| 4 f | 5 e | 6 b |

#### Grammar
B

| | |
|---|---|
| 1 to work | 2 to collaborate |
| 3 coming | 4 Persevering |
| 5 to set | |

### Building Content ❷
p.18

#### Language Patterns
B

| | | |
|---|---|---|
| 1 c | 2 d | 3 f |
| 4 b | 5 e | 6 a |

### Building Content ❸
p.19

#### Reading
**Following the Reading**
1 ~~let the group~~
2 her daughter turned six years old → she got pregnant
3 perfect → healthy, an anxious → a peaceful
4 does yoga → meditates

### Learning How
p.20

A

| | | |
|---|---|---|
| 1 c | 2 d | 3 a |
| 4 b | | |

B
(Example Answer)
Transition 1: To start with, I'd like to define successful leadership for you.

Transition 2: Now that I've defined leadership, I'd like to share my idea of teamwork with you.

Transition 3: Now that I have defined teamwork for you, I want to tell you what I think a successful career looks like.

Transition 4: I've discussed my idea of a successful career, so now, I'd like to summarize today's talk.

### Checklist
p.23

1 By using more precise language, the speech becomes more interesting and coherent for an audience.
2 We should define terms more clearly so that there are not any misunderstandings or confusion surrounding the terms.
3 Transitions separate the body of the speech into manageable pieces.
4 They tell the audience that you are moving from the introduction to main point 1, from main point 1 to main point 2, and so on.

## How to Do Something

### Warm-up
p.24

1 How to buy a used car
2 How to make a salad
3 How to write a résumé
4 How to build a campfire
5 How to set up an aquarium
6 How to use a fire extinguisher

### Building Content ❶
p.25

#### Vocabulary

| | |
|---|---|
| 1 survival | 2 used |
| 3 fire extinguisher | 4 set up |
| 5 résumés | 6 healthfully |

#### Grammar
B

| | | |
|---|---|---|
| 1 must | 2 should | 3 must |
| 4 might | 5 should | |

## Reading

### Following the Reading

1 One of the most important aspects of outdoor survival is building a shelter.
2 You should build your shelter on high ground so that it does not get flooded.
3 It makes the shelter more rain and wind resistant.
4 She witnessed a man choking on a piece of steak.
5 It helps with balance.
6 You should place your hands above the abdomen.

## Learning How     p.28

**A**

| | | |
|---|---|---|
| 1 c | 2 e | 3 b |
| 4 d | 5 f | 6 a |

**B**

(Example Answer)

1 How to go on a date: Have you ever wanted to know how to really impress someone on a first date?
2 How to cook kimchi stew: Last weekend, I prepared the most delicious bowl of kimchi stew for my family.
3 How to raise children: Dr. Phil says, "Do not burden your children with situations they cannot control."
4 How to wash a car: Look at the before picture of my car. This is after a weekend of camping in the rain. Now, look at my car after I washed it.

5 How to do your taxes: (You could begin your speech by gazing at a tax form in one hand and pretending to do calculations on a calculator in the other.) Oh, excuse me. I was just doing my taxes...

## Checklist     p.31

1 It is important so that the audience knows the action being described is advised, necessary, or prohibited.
2 It is important so that the audience knows in which order the actions should occur.
3 The purpose is to grab the audience's attention.
4 The following are mentioned in the unit: a shocking statistic, a rhetorical question, an anecdote, a famous quote, a visual aid, and a gimmick.

# Locations around the World

### Unit 4

## Warm-up     p.32

| | | |
|---|---|---|
| 1 Canada | 2 Italy | 3 South Korea |
| 4 Brazil | 5 India | 6 China |

## Building Content 1     p.33

### Vocabulary

**A**

| | |
|---|---|
| 1 nightlife | 2 coastline |
| 3 blizzard | 4 urban |
| 5 skyline | 6 wedding ceremony |

### Grammar

**B**

| | | |
|---|---|---|
| 1 around | 2 alongside | 3 among |
| 4 along | 5 against | |

## Building Content 3     p.35

### Reading

### Following the Reading

1 American parents have less influence on their children than Asian parents do.
2 In Asia and the Middle East, decisions about career and marriage are strongly influenced by parents.
3 The New York City subway system is fairly loud and dirty, and it lacks basic facilities such as restrooms for passengers.
4 The Seoul and Tokyo subway systems are clean, safe, convenient, expansive, and inexpensive.

## Learning How     p.36

**A**

(Example Answer)

1 Finally, I mentioned the importance of family pets in Southeast Asia.
2 After that, I commented on the average evening meal in Brazil.
3 Then, I discussed some Mexican meals that are simple to make.
4 Ultimately, I told you about three fun locations you can see in London free of charge.
5 After that, I discussed European people's attitudes toward

climate change.

6 I told you about a number of Thai hostels that cost ten dollars or less after that.

7 At the end of my talk, I asked you why Northern Europeans were happier than the rest of the world.

8 I shared with you some information regarding the working conditions of the average Russian twentysomething at the end of my talk.

## Checklist p.39

1 It gives the audience a clearer understanding of each place.

2 Speechwriters often include three main points in the body.

3 The preview of the main points comes at the end of the introduction, and the summary comes at the beginning of the conclusion.

4 The first paraphrasing strategy mentioned is to use words with the same or similar meanings in the new passage (synonyms). The second strategy is to change the word order of the main ideas without changing the meaning of the new sentence.

## Past, Present, and Future — Unit 5

### Building Content ❶ p.41

#### Vocabulary

A

1 20ᵗʰ century
2 ages
3 first
4 modern
5 old-fashioned
6 contemporary

### Building Content ❸ p.43

#### Reading

#### Following the Reading

1 less → more
2 Joe DiMaggio → Roger Maris
3 1970s to the 1980s → 1920s to the 1960s
4 early 20ᵗʰ century → golden age of baseball
5 Hank Aaron → Joe DiMaggio

### Learning How p.44

A

1 b          2 e          3 d

4 c          5 a

## Checklist p.47

1 It gives the audience members a better understanding of the topic.

2 It shows how things have changed over time and how things might change in the future.

3 The interesting details will pique the interest of the audience and draw them into the speech.

4 The summary of the main points and the concluding remarks are the two parts of a speech conclusion.

5 It leaves the audience with a positive lasting impression about the speech.

6 The speechwriter can make a prediction, make a reference to the opening, make a call to action, answer a question that was asked in the opening, or complete a story that was started in the opening.

## Problems and Solutions — Unit 6

### Warm-up p.48

A

1 b          2 a          3 a
4 c          5 c          6 b

### Building Content ❶ p.49

#### Vocabulary

A

1 Racism
2 Income inequality
3 Sexism
4 bullying
5 unemployment
6 obesity

#### Grammar

B

1 where
2 who/that
3 which/that
4 which/that

### Building Content ❸ p.51

#### Reading

#### Following the Reading

1 Poverty can be defined as being under the age of 65 and earning less than $12,500 per year.

2 Universal basic income and a $15 minimum wage were mentioned in the article.

3 He or she would earn about $30,000 per year.

4 They say a $15 minimum wage would hurt small business owners.

**Learning How**                    p.52

A

1 a                  2 b                  3 b

4 a

B

1 Addiction            2 accountable

3 assistance           4 past

5 treatable            6 meaningful

7 likely               8 Summary

## Checklist                    p.55

1 Don't forget to consider problems at the local level.

2 We do this because some audience members might not be familiar with the topic.

3 Each main point in the body should be a solution to the problem.

4 You should use easy-to-read fonts and sizes with key words and sentence fragments. You should use a unified color scheme. You should organize your talking points with bullet points, letters, or numbers. And you should use the slides to deliver the message in your own words.

# Cause and Effect I
Unit 7

## Warm-up                    p.56

1 a                  2 b                  3 b

4 a

**Building Content 1**                    p.57

### Vocabulary

A

1 accomplishment       2 desire

3 frustration          4 devastation

5 satisfaction         6 depression

7 perseverance         8 disappointment

### Grammar

B

1 disappointment

2 satisfaction, accomplish

3 persevere

4 frustration, depression

**Building Content 3**                    p.59

### Reading

**Following the Reading**

1 True                2 False              3 False

4 True

**Learning How**                    p.60

A

1 c                  2 b                  3 d

4 a

B

1

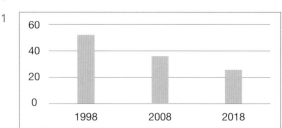

2

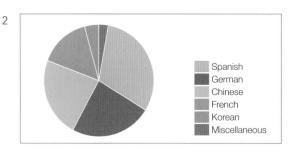

3

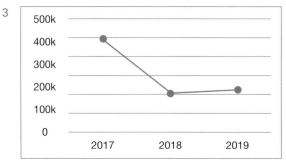

4

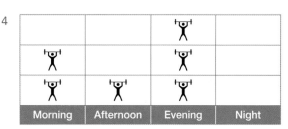

= 20 employees

## Checklist

p.63

1 We can link emotional states to specific causes.
2 We want to clearly communicate to the audience what the cause is and what the effects of that cause are.
3 Good supporting details demonstrate that you are a well-informed speaker and a credible source of the information you are sharing.
4 You are providing the audience with visual cues.

# Cause and Effect II — Unit 8

## Warm-up

p.64

A
1 a          2 b          3 c
4 c

## Building Content ❶

p.65

### Vocabulary

A
1 cancer          2 conflict
3 juvenile delinquency          4 discouraged
5 attributed to          6 insomnia

### Grammar

B
1 much          2 many          3 much
4 many

## Building Content ❷

p.66

### Pronunciation

B
1 /s/          2 /ʃ/          3 /ʃ/
4 /s/          5 /ʃ/

## Building Content ❸

p.67

### Reading

#### Following the Reading

1 homework → parenting
2 the couple as a whole → one person / one person → the couple as a whole

---

3 after → before
4 get divorced → tie the knot

## Learning How

p.68

A
1 d          2 b          3 a
4 c

B
1 a couples therapy
  b conflict resolution
  c assets
  d cease contact
2 a economically stable
  b lower
  c third
  d area
3 a smokers
  b drinkers
  c smokers and drinkers
4 a shareholders
  b board of directors
  c chairperson
  d chief operating officer

## Checklist

p.71

1 It is a good starting point and can lead to a more personal topic for you.
2 *Result from, stem from, be brought about by, be caused by, be produced by,* and *be triggered by* are mentioned in the unit.
3 Each main point in the body of the speech should consist of one of the causes that leads to the effect.
4 The flow chart, organizational chart, Venn diagram, and area chart are mentioned in the unit.

# Group Presentations — Unit 9

## Warm-up

p.72

1 Lecture
2 Business Presentation
3 Demonstration
4 Roundtable Discussion
5 Classroom Presentation
6 Debate

## Building Content ①
p.73

### Vocabulary
A
1 a show of hands
2 an agenda
3 collaborate
4 a compromise
5 a deadline
6 wrap up

### Grammar
B
1 If
2 put
3 will repay
4 If
5 do
6 will not ask

## Building Content ③
p.75

### Reading
**Following the Reading**
1 They stop communicating.
2 They must have defined roles in the group.
3 It lets each member contribute to the presentation in a meaningful way and utilize the talents of the group members.
4 Don't complain about the person to other group members behind his or her back.
5 A good leader should always be conscious of the fact that quieter members of the group might have some wonderful ideas to share.

## Learning How
p.76

A
1 Group Leader
2 Organizer
3 Editor
4 IT Specialist
5 Peacekeeper

## Checklist
p.79

1 *An agenda, compromising, collaborating* are terms related to meetings. (Answers may vary.)
2 It will help the group avoid conflict, save time, and improve the likelihood of creating a high-quality presentation.
3 Group members should communicate, define their roles clearly, pull their own weight, and listen to others.
4 The unit mentions the leader, the organizer, the IT specialist, the editor, and the peacekeeper.

# Challenging a Historical Belief
Unit 10

## Warm-up
p.80
1 f
2 b
3 d
4 c
5 e
6 a

## Building Content ①
p.81

### Vocabulary
A
1 chronicles
2 myth
3 records
4 historians
5 claim
6 descent

### Grammar
B
1 Howard Zinn's
2 Leonardo da Vinci's
3 Quincy Jones's

## Building Content ③
p.83

### Reading
**Following the Reading**
1 False
2 True
3 True
4 False

## Learning How
p.84

A
1 a
2 d
3 e
4 b
5 c

## Checklist
p.87

1 It helps you gain credibility as a speaker.
2 You should begin your argument by expressing opposition to the common belief.
3 The speaker must provide evidence that supports his or her persuasive claim.
4 You can cite your sources during the speech.

# Advistering

## Unit 11

### Warm-up
p.88

A
1 radio spot
2 magazine/newspaper ad
3 flier
4 Internet ad
5 billboard
6 television commercial

### Building Content ❶
p.89

#### Vocabulary

A
1 satisfaction guaranteed  2 durable
3 unique  4 five-star
5 bargain  6 compact

#### Grammar

B
1 should  2 must  3 can

### Building Content ❸
p.91

#### Reading

**Following the Reading**
1 They spend too much time sitting in front of a desk.
2 Their chairs imitate the curvature of the spine.
3 It's healthier to sit with your spine straight and your shoulders back.
4 The writer asks us to imagine a future without back pain.
5 It is a bargain because it costs the same as a typical office chair.

### Learning How
p.92

A
1 c  2 d  3 a
4 e  5 b

B
1 d  2 a  3 b
4 e  5 c

## Checklist
p.95

1 We avoid common adjectives because good descriptors make the item sound more enticing.
2 You must make them realize that life without that product is worse than life with it.
3 It is a five-step method of persuasion.
4 The five steps are grab the audience's attention, establish a need, satisfy the need, visualize the future, and encourage the listeners to take action.

# Making a Change

## Unit 12

### Warm-up
p.96

A
1 d  2 b  3 a
4 c

### Building Content ❶
p.97

#### Vocabulary

A
1 a waste of time  2 take a chance
3 unproductive  4 sedentary
5 doubts

#### Grammar

B
1 I used to be unmotivated, but now I'm motivated.
2 Chen used to be unemployed, but now he has a job.
3 Jim used to waste his time, but now he's productive.
4 Wendy used to live alone, but now she has a roommate.

### Building Content ❸
p.99

#### Reading

**Following the Reading**
1 The author could hear a hint of sadness in her friend's voice.
2 He defined bliss as a career path that satisfied your mind as well as your soul.
3 The author suggests people set short-term goals. The satisfaction from meeting short-term goals will motivate the person to achieve his or her long-term goal.
4 Angela's dream was to become a chef.

A

1 Make the urgency of the situation clear.
2 Make your call to action concise and clear.
3 Make sure you know your audience.
4 Make your call to action easy to perform.

B

| | | |
|---|---|---|
| 1 b | 2 e | 3 c |
| 4 a | 5 d | 6 f |

## Checklist       p.103

1 You use strong commanding language because your purpose is to motivate the audience.
2 A real example can inspire people to change.
3 You should make a call to action.
4 The four elements are make your call to action concise and clear, make your call to action easy to perform, make the urgency of the situation clear, and make sure you know your audience.